To Kenny,
much love &
light,
De

Infinity

A Story of Infinite Love Between Mother and Daughter

Lauren... a beautiful light in so many lives

∞

Inspired and Enlightened by: Lauren M. Kiefer

Written by: Janice Kiefer & Debbie Obradovich

Foreword by Dr. Darren R. Weissman

outskirts press

Denver, Colorado

Infinity
A Story of Infinite Love Between Mother and Daughter
All Rights Reserved.
Copyright © 2012 Janice Kiefer & Debbie Obradovich
v3.0

Outskirts Press, Inc.
http://www.outskirtspress.com

PB ISBN: 978-1-4327-8031-9
HB ISBN: 978-1-4327-8489-8

Outskirts Press and the "OP" logo are trademarks belonging to Outskirts Press, Inc.

PRINTED IN THE UNITED STATES OF AMERICA

This book is dedicated to the eternal life of
Lauren Marie Kiefer

Contents

Preface

On Dec. 25, 2006, Lauren Kiefer was taken from us far too soon. Lauren was a remarkable sister, daughter, granddaughter, niece, cousin, friend and girlfriend. Aside from that, Lauren was a Columbia College graduate; a smart business woman; a fitness queen; a fun-loving party animal; a faithful follower of Christ; a Chicago Cubs fan; a lover of shoes and purses, and a beautiful light in so many lives. We could go on and on...

Lauren had an incredible future ahead of her that she pursued with high hopes. She had so many plans, so many dreams of what could be. We couldn't wait to see what she'd do next. Those of us who knew her can still see her bright smile, still hear her contagious laughter, still hear her say, "HOLLAR!" We are never without her.

We love and miss you, Laur.
Carli

Foreword

We live in a Universe where everything is interconnected. This intelligent web of energy guides the seasons, planets, and stars. But these patterns don't just occur in nature. Every element, cell, organ, gland, and system of the physical body also follows these same natural laws of interconnection.

Take a moment and observe the effect the wind has on the clouds and how it causes a tree branch to sway. Isn't it wondrous how simultaneously we experience this same breeze on our faces? In today's world where we crave signs that there's more to life's circumstances than meets the eye, there already exists a subtle and poetic synchronicity of interconnection that we experience in our daily lives in the most unsuspecting ways.

This dynamic also applies to the concept of life and death. Many people view life as a finite journey, beginning at conception and ending with the final breath. In between, we each encounter the age-old questions: *Who am I? Why am I here? Where am I going?* In our search for answers, we're confronted with the gap between perception and reality. This is particularly true in the face of tragedy.

Challenged by what we *perceive* to be the death of a loved

one, our spirits encounter a crossroad. It's a subtle yet profound moment; a crossroad between breaking and inspiration. One path often leads to inconsolable sadness and hopelessness. The other provides the potential for understanding the *reality* of life and death. It offers each of us an opportunity to truly experience, like the wind, our interconnection with everything. From my own experience, I know the path of inspiration is an epic, transformational journey of awakening to and discovery of life's greatest lesson: Love is infinite.

You hold in your hands the story of two women's epic and transformational journey. Brought together by tragedy, these two mothers chose the path of inspiration. They learned the real and divine message of interconnection and *infinity*, thanks to the assistance of and guidance from the soul of Lauren Kiefer.

Infinity is truly a powerful and enlightening story of love. Love, like energy, has many forms and many expressions. It can't be created, nor can it be destroyed. Like love, *life has no opposite*. There is physical life and non-physical life. Death is the transition between those two worlds. Lauren's beautiful light and her infinite love for her mother couldn't possibly be dimmed by the darkness surrounding her death. Due to Lauren's persistence to reach out, coupled with Debbie Obradovich's selfless act of compassion to help by opening a channel to the non-physical world, the gap between perception and reality was bridged not only for Lauren and her mother, Janice Kiefer, but also for all of us.

I first met Debbie as a client in March of 2004. I knew there was something unique about her. However, it wasn't until I read the manuscript for this book that I realized the magnitude of her uniqueness. She never told me about her ability to act as a medium, a channel for the non-physical world. However, I distinctly remember being filled with such immense emotion while in her presence that it literally brought me to tears. I now have a deeper understanding of and appreciation for why I had those feelings. The depth of love Debbie radiates has the potential to awaken and attract powerful souls. Such was the case for Lauren, and the beginning of a new reality for both Debbie and Janice.

In the Hebrew language wind and spirit share the same word, *ruach*. Denial of our spiritual interconnections or claiming they are illusions is like saying the wind isn't real because we can't see it. To really see, to really feel, to deeply experience all aspects of life, we must be willing to change our perspective and expand our perception. Besides, communication with those in the non-physical world is not a new concept, nor is it uncommon. President Abraham Lincoln was said to have reached out to spiritual mediums during his tenure in the White House to communicate with his 11 year-old son, Willie, who died while he was in office.

It's time to reveal and acknowledge the powerful connection we all share, for ourselves and for the future of our children. By reading this book, I'm certain you'll learn the limitless potential of love's mysterious and miraculous power to bridge the ultimate gap – our perception of interconnection and death – and open the gateway to reality—to *Infinity*.

May the message of this profound book reach your heart and fill your soul with hope and promise. Remember, like love, *life* is infinite.

With Infinite Love & Gratitude-
Dr. Darren R. Weissman
Author, *Awakening to the Secret Code of Your Mind,*
and *The Power of Infinite Love & Gratitude*

Authors' Introduction

From Janice Kiefer:

When I left my home on Christmas Day 2006 to celebrate the holiday with my family, I never could have imagined the horrific tragedy and critical life change that evening would bring. I never guessed that would be the last Christmas I would ever celebrate with my youngest daughter, Lauren, because her life was taken that evening in our home at only 24 years of age.

In this book, you will experience the truly phenomenal, courageous journey Lauren has endured, and how she has come from another place to console and heal me, and to teach others about the beauty and joy of eternal life. This is a true story of pure infinite love between mother and daughter. A love so strong that not even death could destroy.

We would like to share with you the gift of Lauren's amazing journey into infinity.

From Debbie Obradovich:

When I gave birth to my daughters, like all mothers, I envisioned being their teacher and guiding them through life's hurdles and triumphs. Then, unexpectedly and tragically, I lost one of my precious girls. Through her passing, however, she became one of *my* teachers, allowing me to both witness and experience the eternity of her life. It was the experience of my daughter's transition that began the journey that would eventually result in my being able to communicate with Lauren Kiefer, and share her messages of love and hope with Lauren's mother, Janice.

I feel that through Erica's and Lauren's passing, they each in their own way, have left us with an immense legacy of the lessons of love.

Charted in this book are those lessons shared from afar for the reader to contemplate and reflect the meaning in their own lives. We invite you to be aware of your connections to others through the power of love, intuition and your *innate knowing*. You'll be amazed by the journey.

Part I

1

Janice

She came into the world in the middle of the night, took us by storm, deeply touched our lives, and captured our hearts....but left us way too soon.

We drove to the hospital in a blinding snowstorm, hoping to get there before the baby was born. Forty-five minutes after we arrived, a kicking and screaming Lauren Marie Kiefer emerged to take her place in the world. It was Feb. 25, 1982.

"It's a boy!" the doctor said at first, then flipped the baby over. "No, sorry, it's a girl."

There was nothing to be sorry about, as far as I was concerned. Lauren was a beautiful, healthy baby. We quickly learned that her personality rivaled her very vocal arrival.

I could fill this book with chapters about Lauren's very happy childhood and the joy she brought to our lives. Instead, I'll only share a few key stories that will help you get to know who she was, what she valued, and why everyone who knew Lauren loved her so deeply. Don't get me wrong – my daughter wasn't always an angel. But she was always precious and delightful, and Lauren grew up to become one of the bright-est lights in our lives.

❦

My daughter, Carli, was very excited to have a baby sis-ter. She was three-and a-half years-old at the time of Lauren's birth. When I asked Carli's opinion about what to name her sister, she suggested "Moo Moo Cather." I don't know where Carli got that name and I wasn't quite sure what it meant. But even though we didn't use her suggestion, Carli embraced her baby sister with open arms. She soon relinquished her crown as the only princess in our DuPage County, Illinois, household and became quite the mother's helper. Lauren flourished in the spotlight as the new baby.

Shortly after Lauren's birth, her head full of dark hair fell out. Because she was so feisty and bald, we lovingly nicknamed her "Larry." At home, we jokingly referred to her as "our boy." Lauren was bald for two years before her hair grew back; this time it was blonde and so thick that her father had to use a hairbrush nightly to tame the tangles. I still remember Lauren becoming visibly upset whenever she heard someone say, "Get the brush." I can still see her little face, crying with her bottom lip poked out. When Lauren finally had her first salon appoint-ment at the age of three, it took three stylists to detangle her hair.

Lauren soon earned the designation "our little actress" be-cause she acted out at every event. At Carli's First Communion ceremony, for example, I remember Lauren's constant crying. When I later asked her why, she told me it was because, "Carli looks so beautiful." Carli did look beautiful, but I think the real reason for Lauren's tears was that Carli was getting all of the attention that day.

JANICE

When the girls were young, the Christmas holiday was one of our family's favorite celebrations. Lauren would cry and scream whenever we took her to see Santa Claus. She was afraid of him and would refuse to go to bed until I called Santa on Christmas Eve to tell him to leave her gifts and candy on the front porch. Lauren sat next to me intently listening as I made the call. She would only go to bed after I assured her that Santa Claus was not coming into our house.

Carli and Lauren would wake each other on Christmas morning and meet in the bathroom at 3 a.m. I would get up and tell them to go back to sleep because I hadn't heard Santa on the roof yet and there were no gifts on the front porch. It still amazes me how, after all of that, my Lauren grew up to be so feisty and fearless.

During her pre-school years, Lauren starred as the entertainment whenever we gathered at our family's home to eat Christmas dinner and exchange gifts. Every year, Lauren sang her favorite Christmas carol, "The Twelve Days of Christmas." She made us laugh with her own rendition of the song, singing the bridge – "Five golden *wings*" (instead of rings) – at the top of her lungs. She was so special and brought so much joy to our family. Those days were beautiful when the girls were small and our Christmases were merry. Life was so simple.

We took the girls to Disney World when Lauren was three. Disney World was fun, but Lauren, our "little entertainer," was even more fun than the park. While there, she first heard what was to become her favorite song, "That's What Friends Are For," sung by Dionne Warwick. I can still see the audience of tourists gathering around my baby girl as she proudly sang, "That's What Fwends R Fwr." Lauren relished the attention of the crowds as she danced and twirled to the song, her cornsilk-colored hair blowing in the summer breeze. As her parents, we laughed at her antics because we never knew what she would say or do next.

But sometimes Lauren's behavior was embarrassing. Every time we got on the park's monorail, for example, she said aloud, "Moos ovey, Mom you're too fat!" It was amusing to us and to everyone who heard her. I would cringe and turn bright red and all the people around us would laugh. Lauren was such a card.

It was also at age three that Lauren began to establish her own identity, and her feisty, independent nature took root. She began correcting anyone who called her "Laur" or "Laurie."

"My name is Lo…wen," she would say in her loudest voice, unable to pronounce the "r" in the early days of learning to talk. And in case you didn't get it, Lauren would proceed to spell it, loudly enunciating each letter in her own language.

When Lauren was in the second grade we learned how she liked to take charge. She had a way of commanding attention and making her presence known. Lauren portrayed the Cowardly Lion in the school's production of *The Wizard of Oz*. All dressed up in her lion's costume, nothing was going to stop her from being the star of the show. When the boy who spoke right before her didn't recite his lines quickly enough, Lauren grabbed the microphone from his hand and began reciting *her* lines. As she belted out her part, we sank down in our seats filled with both embarrassment and laughter.

In the fifth grade, Lauren fell in love with basketball, especially Michael Jordan and the Chicago Bulls. She even wrote about becoming a star player:

> *"I was daydreaming and fell asleep. I dreamt I was a professional basketball player. I played on the Bulls. I was just as good as everybody on the team. It was the night before the game and the players were talking about how I was*

the only girl on the team. I had to guard Charles Barkley.
'Oh no,' I thought. I talked to Michael, and he said, 'Don't
worry, Lauren. I know you're only 10 years-old, but you
have to play against him.' Michael passed the jump ball
to me and I made a point. Everyone slapped my hands.
We won the game 128-111. After the game, they all had
wine, and I had to have apple juice. 'Wow,' I said. 'What
an amazing dream!'"

Lauren was a little girl with so many hopes and dreams of what her life would be. From that point forward, she pulled her hair tightly into a ponytail and, with braces gleaming, she began her basketball career. She certainly had her share of knocks and bruises. Carli and I thought she was a tomboy and constantly teased her to act more like a girl.

Lauren began to emerge like a butterfly from a cocoon when she graduated from the eighth grade. The braces came off and her ponytail came down. Suddenly, Lauren had curves and nail polish. Although she continued to play basketball, Lauren began to pay attention to her appearance. Sitting on the bench, she would look across the gym to get our attention and mouth: "Does my hair look good?" In response, we would tell her: "Pay attention to the game." Other times, I'd catch a glimpse of her on the bench only to find her checking for broken nails. Lauren became very popular in high school and was voted freshman homecoming queen.

Like all households, the teenage years were wild in our house. By the time she was 14 and Carli was 17, Lauren was thought of as the "annoying little sister." She drove Carli and her friends crazy. They drove me crazy, too, especially when they fought over the telephone – whose turn it was to use the phone or whose turn it was to hang up. I found myself yelling at them in an effort to intervene. But the bickering didn't stop. I thought the girls would carry those grudges forever.

However, if parents are lucky enough to have the opportunity, we get to see our kids grow out of those irrational and annoying phases. As I often predicted would happen, Carli and Lauren became best friends, and Carli's friends soon became Lauren's. I'm fortunate enough to have witnessed my girls grow to the point where they both understood and appreciated having a sister.

As the new phase of their relationship blossomed, it was clear to me that Lauren looked up to Carli and was always excited and honored when her big sister invited her to hang out with their now mutual friends. Lauren solicited Carli's advice and shared her secrets. After Lauren passed, I found her "Vision" essay in one of her school notebooks, which was written in 2005, not too long before she graduated from Columbia College with a bachelors of arts degree in broadcast journalism. When I read it, it seemed to me as though Lauren was summing up her life:

> "I am very close with my sister. Growing up together we have experienced many things, such as my parents' divorce. We became close through this and now we are even closer. She was always the 'golden child' and I was the bad one. But through everything she has never once looked down on me. She taught me not to care if I screwed up, life is filled with mistakes and nobody is perfect. If you asked me five years ago, I would have never thought my sister and I would be so close."

Lauren deeply loved her family. She was very close to my parents, whom she and her sister nicknamed Nani and Baba.

She also loved my sister, Jeanne, whom Lauren and Carli lovingly called DeeDee. Lauren visited Nani and Baba often, even while in college, and she always brought them so much joy. My father loved that Lauren always tweaked his nose, called him cute and referred to him as her boyfriend.

She also wrote about her relationship with our family in her "Vision" essay:

"My grandparents and my aunt are very special to me because they have always been there for me. Whenever I need anything they are always willing to drop what they are doing, and help me out. I can't even tell you how many times my grandpa has helped fix my car, or when I had to drive to far places my aunt always offered to take me. They have been with me from newborn until now. My grandpa is my buddy and we golf together, and I watch soap operas with my grandma. They make me feel special. I have learned to value my family from their generous ways and never take anyone of them for granted."

Lauren reflected on her relationship with her father, Nick, in that essay, and how he helped her learn the importance of taking responsibility:

"My father is also an important person. Growing up he was very strict. Even though I hated his rules, I am grateful because they made me become more motivated to take school more seriously. He also taught me to defend myself. I have seen him work hard and accomplish things he wanted to. I have learned to take responsibility and know that things don't just get handed down to you."

Lauren made all of her friends feel special and she had a unique and close relationship with each one. I used to call them her "partners in crime" because those girls were always up to something. They were loyal to each other, no matter how much mischief they got into. Even Lauren's former boyfriends remained her friends. She was genuine, charming and impossible not to love, and they always kept in contact with her.

Lauren truly understood the value of friends, as she noted in the college essay:

"My life would not be complete without my friends. I feel as though I can trust them and tell them anything. My friends have taught me to listen to my heart. I am lucky to have them in my life. They have seen me at my absolute worst and best."

Many people still remember Lauren's extraordinary zest for life and the way she entered a room with a big smile shouting, "Hollar!" Now, when Lauren's friends visit me, we laugh and cry as we exchange stories about her zany antics: "Remember when Laur did this?" Despite the laughter, we still feel the deepest sense of loss. As I sit with Lauren's friends looking at pictures of her, it's impossible not to imagine how wonderful it would be if she were present and sitting among us. It's impossible not to miss her.

2

Janice

We attended a Catholic church when my daughters were growing up, and I made sure they were present for all of their Saturday morning Catechism classes from the first through eighth grades. But I never thought of us as being overly religious. We attended church to worship God, and we were following family tradition.

When Lauren began attending Columbia College in Chicago, she also started attending Mass during the week in the city. She sometimes attended Mass at our church on weekdays, as well as on Sundays. Lauren was beautiful inside *and* out. There were days when I actually could see a luminous glow around her and others mentioned seeing it, too. Although Lauren didn't talk about the depth of her faith with everyone, she did write about it in the "Vision" college essay:

> "*My faith is very important to me. It upsets me because I didn't go to church on a regular basis until I was 19 years-old. I really never understood until I actually went to church. I can't explain how God has been there for me,*

but He is one of the most important people in my life. He seems to be there when I need Him most. The lesson I have learned is to not rely on God to make my life perfect. Life isn't perfect and if something bad happens to me, I shouldn't get mad or think He isn't watching over me."

❦

Lauren often went to the cemetery to visit and talk to God, and occasionally she brought Him flowers. There was a special crucifix at the cemetery where she sometimes made her pilgrimages. Ironically, she would later be buried parallel to the crucifix.

A few times when Lauren announced her plans to spend time with God I inquired: "Can't you spend some time with your mother?"

I'll never forget the day Lauren stood at our kitchen counter and I saw light radiating around her as she talked. "Mom, you are my best friend," she said, "but God – I can't begin to tell you what He does for me."

I had an awful thought at that moment; a thought I kept to myself: "He's going to love you too much, Laur, and take you away from me." Not too long after that, Lauren told me she wasn't afraid to die.

"Mom, what happens, happens," she declared. "I'm going to live my life. You worry too much. That's why you don't have any fun."

Mothers are made for worrying, I wanted to tell her, but I didn't want to worry her by saying that. I did my best to keep my fears at bay, especially since I didn't truly understand Lauren's growing relationship with God. Looking back, I wonder whether Lauren knew that she wouldn't be here long. Was

God preparing *me* for the time He would take her?

∞

Lauren had a friend, Kate, who didn't believe in God. She found it troubling.

"You never know what could've happened to make a person feel that way," I said in an effort to explain.

"It doesn't matter what happened previously," Lauren replied. "A person only needs to look at all of the miracles around them to know that He exists. I'm going to pray for her."

Two weeks before Lauren passed, she elatedly shared with me that Kate had changed her mind about God. Lauren gave the young woman her own cross pendant; a pendant Kate still proudly wears.

3

Janice

When Lauren was 18, Carli gave her the gift of a session with a professional photographer. I accompanied Lauren to the photo shoot, which was in Chicago.

"Have you ever thought about modeling?" the photographer asked Lauren as he took dozens of pictures of her from multiple angles.

"No," she replied.

Despite her striking beauty and model-like figure, which always garnered a lot of attention, Lauren was very modest. She didn't think she had the physical attributes to pursue a modeling career. As a matter of fact, Lauren laughed about the photographer's inquiry after the session, and made fun of the dramatic poses he requested.

When the collection of photographs arrived at our home, many of the shots were stunning. There was one that was particularly striking – it was of Lauren dressed in a red sweater, posing with her hair in a ponytail. Of course, Lauren thought she looked ugly in that picture. But it was always my favorite photograph and we referred to it as "the red sweater picture."

I convinced her to send several of the photos to a few model-ing agencies. This was a lot of work, but well worth it because Lauren and I had such an unforgettable and fun time together.

To Lauren's surprise, several of the agencies positively re-sponded to her inquiries. She signed with a well-known, Chicago-based agency and they set up another photo session for her in Chicago with a renowned photographer from New York. Of course, I went with Lauren to that session and I was very proud as I watched her pose like a professional in a variety of outfits.

Lauren's composite cards (known as "comp cards" in the modeling industry) were created with photos from this session. A comp card features the model's best headshot, as well as the name and contact information for the agency representing her. Lauren decided to use her first and middle name professionally. I still treasure the comp card I have featuring the angelic face of "Lauren Marie."

Not too long after that photo shoot, Lauren received a tele-phone call from her agent telling her she had been chosen to model hair extensions in New York at the International Beauty Show.

"Mom! Mom!" Lauren ran down the stairs screaming for me. "I'm going to New York!"

"Not without me!" I said.

After convincing Lauren that she wasn't going alone, she let me tag along. We flew to New York for what was to become a whirlwind, five-day trip. On the second day, a representa-tive from a prestigious, Manhattan-based modeling agency approached Lauren. The agent said she could guarantee that Lauren would work as a model every day if she moved to New York.

"Absolutely not," I said when Lauren told me about it that

evening. "Maybe when you're 21 you can move here, but not now. You're too young."

I still remember Lauren being very angry with me. Her eyes filled with tears.

"Don't cry," I said. "Your eyes will get puffy and you won't be able to finish your modeling job."

I think about this incident often. Maybe I should've let Lauren move to New York to pursue a modeling career. Maybe if I had, she'd still be alive today.

Although Lauren wasn't speaking to me after that conversation, we still went to dinner at a nearby restaurant. We were waiting in a long line for a table when a man standing nearby with his friends summoned the host to immediately seat us. We didn't know him and he didn't say anything to us; however, I thanked him as the host escorted us to our table.

Lauren and I ate dinner in silence. I couldn't help but notice that our benefactor was staring at my daughter, which deeply annoyed me and reaffirmed my position that Lauren was not moving to New York. I became angrier the longer I sat watching that man stare at Lauren. He even approached our table just as we finished eating.

"Mom, your daughter is gorgeous," he said, still staring at Lauren.

"Thank you," I replied curtly, my tone turning sharper. "But if you ever get near her you'll have to deal with me."

"The desire to protect your daughter and your feisty spirit are admirable," he said. He winked at me. I watched him walk away from our table. He held in his hands behind his back a vanity license plate. It said "Sopranos." Although I wasn't a big television viewer, it suddenly dawned on me that the man who had helped us secure our table and who had been staring at Lauren was actually an actor on the TV series "The Sopranos."

My daughter and I had a good laugh about it as we walked out of the restaurant.

❦

My decision not to let Lauren move to New York didn't stop her modeling career. She appeared in print advertisements for a few major department stores and also had a few runway experiences. We even took a trip to Hawaii where Lauren modeled swimsuits with pristine beaches as the backdrop. Often, we were either on a plane, a train or in a taxi running to jobs or modeling auditions, which are called "go-sees."

"Where are you taking me now?" I'd always ask Lauren every time we began a new adventure. We'd laugh because neither of us could believe the incredible opportunities resulting from Carli's photography gift. We became very close as a result of those times together, creating beautiful memories that I will forever treasure.

Poise and grace weren't Lauren's strongest attributes. We often laughed that clumsiness was in her genes – she took after me and Nani. Lauren sometimes fell down the stairs at home; tripped over something, or frequently bumped in to stationary objects.

When Lauren was chosen to do a runway show at the Hyatt Regency Hotel in Chicago, I was a little nervous. I wasn't sure if she could manage walking down a runway in three-inch heels while photographers snapped pictures and 3,000 people watched her. However, I knew my mission was to encourage her, not share my misgivings.

"I know you can do it, sweetheart." I told Lauren before the show. "I'm sure you'll be fine."

I sat in the audience and watched that skinny little girl dressed in a 40-pound, beaded, Asian-inspired wedding gown, gracefully walk down the runway, turning pirouettes. She was so poised and beautiful, I found myself crying in disbelief.

"Is that really Lauren?" I asked my friend seated next to me.

Lauren was so excited after the show and so was I because my little girl's dream had come true.

Soon after the runway show, Lauren's agent began regularly calling our house in an effort to convince her to do a "go-see" for a group of Japanese agents traveling to Chicago in search of new talent. Some famous models began their careers in Japan. If Lauren was chosen, she would have to live and work there for a minimum of two months. Despite the assurances from the agent that Lauren had "what it takes" to work in Japan, I had many misgivings. I knew I wouldn't be able to take two months off work to move to Japan with her, and I was certainly opposed to sending her alone. Even though I knew I wouldn't let Lauren go to Japan, I agreed to let her go through with the audition.

Lauren was attending day classes at Columbia College in Chicago at the time. She told me the appointment with the Japanese agents was after class at the Belmont Hotel. We agreed she would call me when she finished so that I could pick her up. By 8:30 that evening, I still hadn't heard from Lauren and I was beside myself with worry. My sister, Jeanne, picked me up and we began driving to Chicago. I was determined to find Lauren, even though I didn't know the location of the hotel. We were almost downtown when my cell phone rang. Thankfully, it was Lauren.

"Where are you, Laur?" I asked excitedly. That was the only question I got to ask before Lauren began pouring out her story.

"Mom, my wallet was stolen at school today. I didn't have any money to take a taxi to the hotel so I got on a bus. The driver felt sorry for me and let me ride for free. I didn't know which stop to get off. I got off a few blocks from school, only to discover that there is no Belmont Hotel. I kept walking. Suddenly, I looked up and saw the Tremont Hotel, so I went in and it was the right place."

That was my Lauren, full of stories, always flying by the seat of her pants, always on a new adventure that could only happen to her.

"Don't move," I told her, feeling indescribable relief. "We'll be there in a few minutes."

During the rest of that week, the modeling agent for the Japanese market continuously called our house, to discuss Lauren's future career in Japan. However, I discouraged the agent because I had no intentions of letting her go. Besides, I felt Lauren would be hesitant to leave her friends and family for such a lengthy stay in a foreign country.

There was a part of me who was afraid of the lurking dangers in the world that Lauren sometimes seemed too naïve to notice. That part of me wanted to keep her locked in her room until she turned 30. On the other hand, I always encouraged Lauren to go for what she wanted in life. I told her she could accomplish anything she wanted because she had the "world by the ass."

After two years, Lauren decided that the modeling business wasn't for her. She didn't think her skin was "tough enough," and she decided she no longer wanted to pursue a modeling career. To Lauren, modeling was just a fun thing to do. In the end, I had no regrets. I saw how much Lauren had matured as a result, and I was grateful for how beautifully my baby girl was growing up. Lauren graciously thanked me for all the experiences we had and, to my delight, she wrote about our relationship in her "Vision" essay:

JANICE

"My mother is my best friend. From the moment I can remember until now, she has never left my side. She is one of the most caring and strongest persons I know. She has taught me a great deal and I feel what I have learned from her has helped me become who I am today. She has taught me to believe in myself, even when times were rough. She always told me I had the world by the ass and I could accomplish anything. She always tells me that she knows I will do well. She taught me to have manners and respect others. But most important she taught me that things don't come easy sometimes and life is hard work. I look up to her and respect her for everything she has accomplished in her life."

4

Janice

Carli, Lauren, and I went to late afternoon Mass on Christmas Eve 2006. Despite the gloomy weather, I was happy. I felt so lucky and blessed to have my two precious daughters seated next to me. The girls were excited to be able to spend time together. They had so much to talk about that I had to remind them to be quiet in church.

"Shhhh," I whispered. "How old are you two?"

I glanced over at Lauren as she and Carli settled into their seats. I smiled when Lauren's leopard heels caught my eye because I knew how much she loved her shoes.

When we returned home, other family members began to arrive. Celebrating Christmas Eve after Mass was an important tradition in our family, a tradition handed down by my grandmother. Since 2003, the celebration had been held at our house. More than 20 aunts, uncles, cousins, grandparents and close friends gathered to eat and share lots of laughter.

As I look back, I remember my mood suddenly changed in the evening. I didn't understand it since all of the people I loved were there and everyone was having such a great time.

Maybe I was finally beginning to pay attention to the feelings of impending doom that had been haunting me for months.

✌∂∾

The feeling of doom first arrived when I received a life-sized copy of the "red sweater picture" of Lauren from the photographer whose photos launched her modeling adventures. Even though it was my favorite photo of Lauren, as I unrolled the poster a horrifying thought crossed my mind: *This photo looks as if it belongs over a casket.* I was immediately alarmed. I rolled up the poster and slid it behind my living room couch.

The dread returned every time I touched the poster, so I only moved it occasionally. All the while I kept telling myself to stop being an over-protective mother and let Lauren live her life. The last time I moved the poster was two months before Lauren's passing. Holding it in my hands, the frightening feelings were stronger than ever. I even had the thought, "It's getting closer."

Two weeks before that fateful Christmas Day in 2006, as I got dressed for work, I couldn't resist the urge to peek into Lauren's room. She was sleeping so peacefully. Her foot was dangling from under the covers. I went in and kissed it.

"Mom, what are you doing?" she asked groggily.

"Honey, I just love you," I replied, bending down to kiss her forehead.

As I stood up, I was nearly overcome by the feeling, "It's getting closer." I knew immediately that this thought was more than motherly worry and anxiety. I did my best to stave off the growing panic gripping my gut. But I felt helpless. I knew I couldn't keep Lauren home from work, and I couldn't make her live in a protective bubble. After all, at age 24 she was an adult. Even today, I'm still not sure I could've done anything differently that would have or could have saved her life.

⌒⌒

I missed most of the family's conversation on Christmas Eve because I was in the kitchen organizing dinner and putting food on the table. I did peek out of the kitchen briefly. Carli and Lauren were entertaining their younger cousins. No matter how old my daughters were, they always made time to play with their younger cousins as if they were their peers. The children's laughter filled our house.

Although I would've preferred to have been a part of all of the fun festivities instead of working in the kitchen, I consoled myself with the reminder that I would be on vacation for the next two weeks. There would be plenty of time to spend with Carli and Lauren. We had already planned our shopping expeditions, and I knew there'd be time for mother-daughter conversations over lunch.

After dessert, we all filed into our family room for the annual exchange of gifts. The Christmas tree sat next to the window, beautifully decorated with ornaments depicting my daughters' childhood adventures. I had given my girls an ornament every year on the day we decorated our tree, and from each branch dangled many memories amidst the twinkling lights.

Carli and Lauren always opened their gifts to each other first while I took photos. I always marveled at my daughters' closeness, and they were the most precious and treasured gifts I had ever received. Lauren squealed with excitement as she slipped out of her leopard heels to try on the pair of red, patent-leather high-heels Carli gave her. I remember her beaming smile as she pulled out the Nike sweats and matching running shoes I gave her. Shoes of any type were perfect gifts for Lauren, especially since she was known for owning shoes to match every outfit.

My father was so delighted with his presents that he sounded like a little boy when he exclaimed, "Why do you guys buy me so many gifts? You should save your money."

My mom also was happy to receive so much attention and so many wonderful presents. Her health was failing and we accurately predicted that it might be her last Christmas with us.

I usually waited until the family finished opening their gifts before opening mine. Not just because I was the photographer – I truly enjoyed watching everyone's excitement as they unwrapped and opened their presents.

Opening Lauren's gifts to me always involved a special ritual. That Christmas, the ritual began the beginning of December. Lauren finished her shopping early, wrapped her presents and placed them under our tree. For nearly a month, I had been picking up the box labeled "Mom" and shaking it.

"Don't peek," Lauren admonished me.

"I won't Laur," I promised. "But it looks expensive. What is it?"

"You'll have to wait until Christmas," she replied. "But that's all you're getting from me."

"You shouldn't have spent so much money on me," I said laughing. I just knew she had gone way over her budget.

On Christmas Eve, as I sat on the stairs of our family room, I discovered the gift was a diamond "journey" necklace. I could feel Lauren watching me open her gift. Even in the midst of all the noisy voices and the crunch of wrapping paper, we were able to have a special moment that I will always treasure.

Lauren walked up the steps behind me and told me to take off the "Circle of Love" necklace she had given me the previous Christmas. She placed the journey necklace around my neck. When I opened the beautiful greeting card she gave me, Lauren took it from my hand. Looking at me, she read the card aloud. The card was about angels and very special love, and how earth angels help us to become happy. Lauren said whenever she thought about angels she thought about me, because I always looked out for her; loved her and brightened her life. Little did I know at the time that Lauren was preparing me for the journey of my life, and that she would be the one looking out for, taking care of, and guiding me.

5

Janice

Christmas Day began as a normal day for Lauren and me. She drove to our favorite coffee shop, as she did on most days, returning with a large cup of coffee, super-charged with a double espresso for her, and a regular, medium-sized cup for me. We engaged in our morning "coffee talk." I don't recall anything we shared, even though I really wish I could. Nonetheless, I'm so grateful that we were able to share our morning routine together. When we finished our coffee, Lauren got up from the kitchen table.

"I'm going to church, Mom," she yelled as she bounded up the stairs.

I was surprised since we had all gone to Christmas Eve Mass. But I decided to stay home. I was still exhausted from the party that didn't end until midnight.

"I'm sitting on this couch and not moving until we go to Carli's for dinner," I told Lauren when she returned downstairs dressed and ready to leave. Even though the house was a mess, with wrapping paper, dishes, and remnants of Christmas Eve cheer strewn everywhere, I decided I deserved a rest. I intended to give the house a good cleaning the day after Christmas, unaware of the looming nightmare and critical life change that evening would bring.

❧❀❧

Lauren picked up a pie from the home of Carli's friend then drove her own car to her sister's to help with the Christmas dinner preparations. Carli later told me about Lauren's silly antics while peeling potatoes, sometimes letting them fall in the garbage can. Their conversation had been casual and light, Carli shared, and she was glad they had an opportunity to spend some time alone together.

I remember leaving our house around 1:30 p.m. I closed the blinds so that no one could see the Christmas tree and gifts. I left lights on in the family room and kitchen and I recall checking the front door's lock twice.

Carli prepared a lovely Christmas dinner and we gathered around her dining room table to eat. Lauren always sat next to me at our family gatherings, and if anyone took her seat next to me she had me ask them to move. I remember she was unusually quiet, but I don't recall being alarmed since we all tended to talk at once during our holiday dinner celebrations.

When we finished eating, Carli and I cleared the table and started washing dishes. Lauren's dad accompanied her to put air in her tires, which also gave him the opportunity to be alone with her. When they returned, it was time for dessert and there was my Lauren sitting next to me again. I recall looking at her beautiful face and thinking to myself: "Her nose is perfect; she is such a beauty." I still have that image of her in my mind.

All our festivities ended at approximately six that evening and Lauren announced that she was going home. This is where I wish I could change the ending of this chapter; rewrite the horrendous story of this moment in our lives. How I wish I had asked Lauren to come home after church to pick me up. In that way, we would have been driving home from Carli's in the same car.

After Lauren kissed everyone good-bye, I thought, "I don't have to worry about you tonight; you're just going home." Where was my "mother's intuition" at that moment? I had no awful feeling; no negative thoughts, no whispering voices demanding that Lauren stay and wait for me. I watched her leave while I stayed at Carli's to be with my mom so Jeanne could drive our uncle home. I can still see Lauren walking out of the door that evening.

We lived only a few miles from Carli – just minutes away by car. I'm certain I left Carli's house and headed home about 7 p.m., which means Lauren was alone no more than an hour before I arrived. Lauren's car was parked in the driveway when I pulled mine next to hers. The overhead garage door was open and the garage lights were on. The door to the house's lower level was wide open, which was the first sign that something was wrong. Lauren never entered the house that way because the only automatic garage door opener was in my car.

I jumped out of my car, ran through the garage and into the house. From the moment I entered, every nerve in my body was on edge. I ran down the stairs to the family room, frantically calling, "Laur, Laur, are you here?" She did not answer. My stomach turned somersaults as I ran up the stairs from the family room to the foyer. When I got to the top, I discovered what no parent should ever have to find; what no human being should ever have to witness. My love, my child, my precious Lauren was lying face down by the front door

"Oh my God!" I screamed, as I ran to her. "My precious Lauren!"

I knelt down beside my daughter and grabbed her wrist hoping to find a pulse as I examined her closely. I'm sure my sweet child was trying to get out of the house as she was viciously assaulted with a baseball bat. I knew in that instant that there was no possible way for her to still be alive. I remember kissing her cheek. But I didn't realize at the time that would be the last kiss I would ever be able to give her. I regret to this day not lying down beside Lauren and cradling her in my arms until the authorities arrived to remove her body from our home.

I jumped up from the floor and frantically began searching for the phone. When I found it, I dialed 9-1-1. "My daughter is dead!" I screamed at the woman who answered. She began asking me a series of questions none of which seemed relevant to me at the time. "Just get here," I yelled and hung up.

In the midst of the events that I can only describe as surreal, I realized that I needed to call Carli. How could I tell her what I knew would change her life forever? What words could I use to explain that her only sibling had been murdered in our house? Carli and her sister had become so close...we had all just spent a lovely Christmas together at Carli's home.

I don't know how I managed to dial Carli's number. As soon as she answered the phone I blurted out: "Lauren is dead!" I can't even remember the rest of our conversation. Looking back, I wish I had handled that call better even though I know during a situation like that there was no "better" option.

I called my parents, sister, and Nick. Then I covered the body of my sweet and beautiful baby daughter with an afghan and said to her, "I can't help you anymore, sweetheart."

I ran out of the house. When I got outside, the ambulance was in my driveway; the station was located across the street. One of the firemen we had known for years was also standing in my driveway. I ran crying to him.

"My girl is dead," I sobbed.

I remember his attempt to comfort me although few words were spoken. I'm sure he was in shock, too. As the fireman walked me across the street and escorted me to a private room in the station, I also remember thinking of my sweet Carli and my elderly parents. Knowing how they must be feeling and what they were going through, made the situation even more unbearable for me.

My family arrived and was escorted to the room where I was waiting. As they sobbed and held on to each other, I paced back and forth throughout the fire station in disbelief. How did this happen? How could this happen in our neighborhood? What kind of sick maniac would do this? Adrenaline took over as I paced. There was a part of me that wanted to jump out of my skin…run away…escape the situation. I could not believe – I did not want to believe – Lauren would never be coming home again. I wanted to turn back the clock to our wonderful family dinner and erase the unbearable scene I had just discovered in the foyer of our home.

I know now that I had to disengage at that moment in order to withstand the crushing tide of emotion and grief rising to pull me under. But that detachment did nothing to blunt the seething anger or the excruciating pain. There are no words to describe my emotions.

∽∾

Although it seemed as if we were waiting at the fire station for hours, I really don't know how long it took DuPage County deputies to swarm our neighborhood. A female detective entered the room where we were sequestered. Her name was Tiffany. As I was to learn, Tiffany was a compassionate woman who would become my ally, confidant and friend in the ensuing months. But in the moments following her introduction, forging an alliance was the last thing on my mind as Tiffany began the preliminary stages of the investigation.

"Why are you asking all these questions?" I snapped. "The answers won't change anything. The answers won't bring Lauren back!"

I was so angry at that moment; I didn't care about "who," "what" or "why." The enormity of the situation felt incomprehensible. But I was fully aware of the facts: my daughter was dead and she was not coming back to me.

Tiffany allowed us to leave after what seemed like hours of questioning. I recall walking out of the fire station that evening feeling empty and without direction. On Christmas Day 2006, my life changed forever. Not only did I lose my precious daughter, I lost my home and my sense of purpose in life.

I went to Carli's house that night, which was the beginning of my living with her for the next few months. Despite her own grief, Carli opened her heart to take care of me. I was never alone. Many friends also banded together to support me and my family as we waited for answers from the authorities investigating Lauren's death.

❦

News about Lauren's death sent shock waves throughout DuPage County and surrounding communities, and was the headline story in all of the news reports. Although it was hard for Carli and me to fully comprehend our unimaginable loss, reality set in the next day as droves of friends and neighbors began arriving at my daughter's home to express sympathy and share their feelings of disbelief, disgust, and anger.

"Who would hurt Lauren?" they asked. "She was so beautiful and genuine. Everyone loved her."

We spent the next two days in a fog as we prepared for Lauren's services. I remember feeling inexpressibly and miserably sick; a feeling I hope to never experience again. I didn't realize until the day of Lauren's wake how many people knew and loved her. It was unbelievably gratifying and simultaneously heart-wrenching to talk to the hundreds of people who stood in line for two hours to pay their respects.

A team of DuPage County Sheriff's detectives also attended Lauren's wake. They sat in the front row observing people as they offered condolences to me and my family. As I was to later learn, they were observing their primary suspect, who had the audacity to attend the wake.

I can still recall the killer's cold eyes as he leaned in to tell me his name. I can't and won't speak his name or see it in print in proximity to my daughter's. Although he said he was sorry for our loss, he did not exhibit the least bit of remorse. I remember overhearing him ask Carli if she remembered him as he introduced himself. He told her Lauren had been a childhood friend. At that moment we would have had no reason to suspect him. I remembered later that Lauren, the child who loved everyone, had befriended him in elementary school when he and his family moved to our neighborhood from another country. He even played at our house when they were kids. But after grade school, Lauren and her friends lost contact with him, and as far as I knew, she never saw or heard from him again. This horrible person never crossed my mind again until I was faced with the reality that he had wantonly taken my daughter's life.

I was later told by the detectives that the killer had been scouting our neighborhood Christmas Day. He had called friends seeking money. According to telephone records, he even called our house while we were at Carli's. We're not sure how long he had been in our house before Lauren arrived home. I know $300 was missing from my nightstand. If it were truly a burglary and I had walked in while he was there, I would've given him everything I owned in order to save Lauren's life.

〜⁂〜

I got out of bed very early and quickly dressed the morning of Lauren's funeral. I didn't care how I looked. I was in a fog, and just going through the motions. I got into my car and began driving to the funeral home, oblivious to my surroundings. I was determined to get to the funeral home before people began to arrive so that I could spend time alone with Lauren.

I don't recall what made me look up as I was driving in a daze, but I noticed a local restaurant's marquee just as I was passing it. It read: "Lauren, you will be dearly missed." It occurred to me that the whole town was in mourning.

I believe it was the state of shock and disbelief that allowed me to walk alone into the room containing Lauren's casket. Although I had imagined spending this time alone with her, I found myself captivated by all of the beautiful flowers, photos and keepsakes scattered around the room. I picked up a small teddy bear with angel wings. Clutching the bear to my heart, I had to sit down before I fainted. Red roses and a ribbon were sewn along its head in the exact location where Lauren had been injured. The funeral director and one of his employees entered the room to check on me. I showed them the teddy bear and they were as amazed as me. I later learned that the bear had been sent by one of Lauren's friends, who had no idea of the location of Lauren's injury.

Family and friends began to arrive. I sat dazed in the front row, oblivious to what was going on around me. I felt emotionally detached, as if it were a stranger's service rather than my own daughter's. As Lauren's still-favorite song, "That's What Friends Are For," was played. I sat weeping and clutching the angel teddy bear. Lauren always planned to have that song played at her wedding. I never ever imagined that instead it would be played at her funeral.

Part II

Part V

6

Debbie

On the morning of Dec. 26, 2006, I was watching the television news when a disturbing report was broadcast: A 24-year-old woman had been killed in her home on Christmas. Having my own 26-year-old daughter, my heart immediately grieved for the young woman, and her mother, whom I knew was coping with a senseless and unbearable loss.

Over the next two days, friends and neighbors talked about the death of Lauren Kiefer. Like me, they were concerned because Lauren's home was located in a suburb adjacent to ours. Was there a murderer running loose in our backyards? Were we safe?

The emotion of the situation was compounded by the fact that my friend, Jeff, told me he had heard Lauren worked at a local pub in *our* town. She worked there part-time while attending college. Jeff suddenly turned to me and suggested I use my abilities as an intuitive to help the police.

"You could probably get a description of the murderer or help discover the motive," he said.

I shook my head. It was too close to home for comfort. My

life, even my daughter's life, could be in danger. Besides, what would the police think if I came forward with "inside" information? Would they wonder if I had something to do with it? I was also fearful because the perpetrator was still at-large.

"How would you feel if it were your daughter?" Jeff said, further prodding me. "This guy is at-large and your daughter and other women are still vulnerable."

Although I was annoyed at the time, today I'm extremely grateful that Jeff was relentless in his efforts to push me to take action. Five days after Lauren's death, once again I saw a photo of her during a television news broadcast. The reporter talked about Lauren's background as a student at Columbia College, and that authorities had not yet apprehended the perpetrator. I thought my heart would burst as the reporter noted the seemingly slow pace of the investigation. At that moment, I knew I needed to help.

⁓◈⁓

I'm not a professional intuitive or psychic medium. I taught first grade for nine years. Today, I make my living as a real estate agent. Not many people know about my intuitive abilities: my ability to see, hear and feel past, present and future events. To tell you the truth, I'm not one hundred percent comfortable going public now. But the lessons I've learned as the result of the experiences I've had with the Kiefer family are too important not to share.

Intuition is a gift we *all* possess. It's often referred to as the sixth sense. It's a knowing or perceiving that many people most notably experience as a gut reaction they may not always acknowledge. Sometimes intuitive gifts are hereditary, or nurtured and developed. In other cases, knowing is borne of trauma or tragedy. In my case, I think it was probably a combination of all of my life's experiences that helped me become aware of and accept my gifts.

As a child, I had intuitive or psychic medium experiences and often knew about events days or weeks before they occurred. I often said to my mother, "Grandma visited me today," and many of my relatives who had passed would often spend time with me. It was commonplace for members of my extended family to ask whether I had experienced any recent visitors and inquire about what they had to say. No one, to my knowledge, ever questioned my intuitive abilities, and I felt very comfortable knowing that my relatives who had passed were always near.

As an adult, I had several experiences that allowed me to transform and grow in the understanding of my intuitive abilities. Today, I know those experiences are at the heart of how I came to *know* Lauren and her mother, Janice. For you to understand why you're holding this book in your hand, it's important that I first share those experiences with you.

7

Debbie

In 1979, my first daughter, Erica, was prematurely born. She lived for three-and-a-half months in the neo-natal intensive care unit of Lutheran General Hospital. After contracting spinal meningitis while in the hospital, she lost her brave battle for life without ever coming home.

The night before Erica's passing, the nursing staff said she was stable and that we should go home and get some rest. I had no idea Erica's passing would transpire just hours later. I remember not being able to sleep and getting up to sit in the room that was to become Erica's nursery when she came home. As I sat there worrying about her, the strangest feeling came over me. I felt an overwhelming euphoria; a deep sense of peace flooded through me. I witnessed and felt an incredible light that I can now only describe as a transformational feeling. I knew at that moment, Erica's soul had passed.

A few minutes later, about 4 a.m., the hospital called. "Erica's not doing well," the nurse said. "You and your husband should come back right away."

As my husband and I rushed in our car to the hospital, I

contemplated what I had witnessed in her room. Although I felt as if Erica had already passed, I had no idea what to expect when we arrived at the neonatal intensive care unit.

⸱⸱⸱

The fluorescent lights and constant hum of the machines met us as soon as we stepped off the elevator. The nurses, who had been a steady source of support, looked somber as we walked towards Erica's incubator. We were immediately met by a doctor.

"Your daughter is gravely ill and will likely not live much longer," I remember him saying. "There's no brainwave activity after the high fever. You should consider taking her off life support and letting her go."

I'm not sure if it was me or my husband who asked the doctor whether he was sure about Erica's prognosis, even though I knew in my heart she was already gone. I also don't recall how long my husband and I talked before we agreed to have the life-support equipment removed.

My husband said good-bye to Erica before the doctor disconnected the tubes and machines. He told me he could not watch our daughter die. One of the nurses then escorted me to a private room where I sat in a rocking chair singing softly to my baby. Erica's tiny hands and feet were no bigger than half my little finger, and yet every ounce that she gained during those three months was a triumph. What stands out most in my memory of this gut-wrenching, yet life-changing experience, is holding my daughter in my arms for the first time unencumbered. There were no gloves, tubes or machines preventing Erica from feeling my touch or my eternal love for her.

Despite having witnessed the transition of Erica's spirit earlier that morning, my final moments with my daughter were both beautiful and peaceful. I experienced deep comfort in knowing that she had passed both spiritually and physically bathed in love and light.

Teilhard de Chardin, a famous French scientist and philosopher, once said: "We are not human beings having a spiritual experience. We are spiritual beings having a human experience." As I reflect on my experience with Erica's transition, I became aware of the limitless boundaries of the human soul and spirit, even if I didn't have the words at the time. I learned our bodies are the vessels for the countless journeys of our spirit, and when we shed that vessel, life takes on new dimensions.

8

Debbie

I became interested in learning an ancient healing art known as Reiki, and began taking classes at the College of DuPage in 2000. Reiki, which is pronounced "rākē," originated in Japan The word literally means "universal life force energy." It's a healing technique based on the principle that the therapist can channel energy into the patient by means of touch, which activates the natural healing processes of the client's body and restores physical and emotional well-being.

During a traditional Reiki session, the client lays fully clothed on a massage table. The session involves working on the seven main energy centers, or vortices, of the body known as chakras. Each chakra represents a location through which energy enters and leaves the body. The chakras correspond to specific structural, biochemical and emotional functions of the body. In addition, they are the storehouse of a person's life experiences, which are downloaded on the body's bio-computer and stored in the chakras as subconscious emotions.

I took Reiki classes for one year, while still working as a real estate agent, until I reached the level of Reiki Master. During the training, I discovered that the chakras were a gateway for me to intuitively "hear" and "see" images of people, past or present events, and tune in to specific images and emotions impacting the health or stress level of the client.

I once asked my instructor if this was a common occurrence during a Reiki session. "Generally not," she told me. "You must have a special gift."

Learning Reiki opened a new window of intuitive insights for me. In hindsight, I now understand that my discovery of Reiki was no accident. *Reiki found me* and would serve as the medium for eventually helping others on a deeper level with my intuitive abilities.

⌒◦◡

After a year of practice, I began performing Reiki energy work at a friend's physical therapy business. Because I continued working full-time selling real estate, I saw clients on a limited basis. Nonetheless, the sessions were rewarding – the clients seemed to benefit from the stress relieving qualities of the energy work as well as the intuitive insights that emerged.

During the sessions, I witnessed past or present events and circumstances impacting my client's life and I shared the visual images or auditory messages I received. The energy work was able to help them understand how these events impacted them on an emotional, physical and spiritual level. More and more, my clients began to describe these sessions as a window into their lives, and they would leave my office in a state of peace with enhanced well-being.

During one session with a new client named Vickie, I received an auditory message that seemed separate from her energy. Because the voice was critical and pointed, I first asked Vickie whether she wanted to hear this message, and she agreed.

"You think you are so fancy with the expensive jewelry and all," I said, speaking for the voice I was hearing.

"That's my mother," Vickie responded immediately. "She's deceased. But that's how she always talked to me."

Then the tone and the content of the message suddenly changed. Vickie's mother apologetically acknowledged that she had been an alcoholic and her life had been out of control. She admitted being abusive and noted that she had not been a good mother. Vickie listened intently for a few minutes.

"May I say something to my mother?" she inquired.

"I've never mediated a conversation with the other side before," I replied, "but I'll do my best."

"I love you, Mom," Vickie said.

"Honey, I love you, too," the mother responded through me.

When the session ended, Vickie told me something that helped me immensely. "When you shared the messages from my mother, I heard *her voice*, not yours; even my mother's southern accent."

I don't know how else to describe it other than to say I realized that my intuitive abilities had expanded to incorporate channeling. The best analogy to describe channels is to compare them to telephone wires – the information or signal moves through unfiltered. It bypasses personal beliefs, logic, consciousness and the rational mind. From my side of the experience, channeling feels as if I'm a receiver of what I hear, see and feel, which I then relay in messages to the client.

Days later, Vickie called to tell me that communicating with her mother had helped her further heal some deep wounds. As I hung up the telephone, I felt blessed to be able to facilitate such a profound transformation. Despite the fact that these channeling sessions were very emotional for Vickie, as well as for me, she subsequently found them always deeply healing.

To be able to actually provide my client with a direct link to their loved ones was an incomprehensible gift. Instead of fearing this new discovery of my expanding capabilities, I embraced it; I felt honored to be able to deliver messages of hope and healing.

∽∂∽

It has been scientifically documented that the energy emitted from a Reiki practitioner's hands vibrates at a higher rate than someone who is not attuned to Reiki. It's this higher vibration that the energy of a transitioned soul or spirit can access. This was reaffirmed for me when my Uncle Marvin passed a few years after I first began practicing Reiki. My uncle came often to visit me, but never sought to use me as a channel. I simply felt his energy in my environment. But several years later, a family crisis ensued. During this crisis, I sensed Uncle Marvin's energy, but it was more intense than previous visits. I intuitively felt I needed to channel his message from afar. I opened the Reiki channel and recorded a very emotional session with him. He shared a beautiful message of healing and advice for the entire family. I transcribed Uncle Marvin's message and sent it to everyone even though I risked some of my relatives thinking I was meddling in their affairs. Still, I hoped my uncle's words would be taken to heart.

Later, many family members said the message sounded like my uncle and that they would do their best to heal the conflict. To my surprise, those who were skeptics acknowledged that the words were wise and beneficial, even if they didn't believe the message was from Uncle Marvin.

9

Debbie

In the fall of 2001, my Reiki work led me on an unexpected journey that would become the next step of my awakening to my intuitive abilities and gifts. The experience involved my friends, Mike and Deb, and their now 19-year-old son, Kyle.

When Kyle was a toddler, his parents confided in me that he was not developing like other children his age; not only did Kyle not talk, he did not make eye contact. After several visits to the doctor and numerous tests, Kyle was diagnosed with severe autism. Although the causes of autism are fiercely debated, its effects are not. Children diagnosed with autism invariably have neural development issues; they have limited social and communication skills, as well as restricted and repetitive behavior.

During my occasional visits to Kyle's home, it was always heart-wrenching to witness the difficulties the entire family encountered as they attempted to help Kyle cope with autism. He couldn't talk, so he was unable to make his needs known. He rarely slept through the night. Often Kyle was violent, inflicting pain upon himself and others. It was clear that Mike and

Deb, as well as their other two children, were all experiencing severe stress.

One evening while talking on the telephone with Kyle's mother, I sensed that she was at the breaking point. For the first time, Deb mentioned placing Kyle, who was then almost nine years old, in a home for disabled children. Deb said the home might be the only way she could salvage what was left of her compromised family life. It felt like a plea for help from a desperate mother who was being forced to make difficult choices because she had run out of options. As a mother who once had to make an extremely painful choice about the fate of my child, I understood Deb's pain. Looking back, I now believe it was my own experience that opened the deep well of compassion in my heart and sparked the events that followed.

I had previously learned from my colleagues who were long-time Reiki practitioners that energy work was very helpful for children diagnosed with autism. On the day after Thanksgiving in 2001, and with his parents' permission, I performed a Reiki session while Kyle lay across my lap in the quiet of his room. After a while, he relaxed and fell asleep. I covered Kyle with a blanket and left him peacefully sleeping in his bed.

When I returned to the dining room where Mike and Deb were waiting, they couldn't believe Kyle was asleep. His mother told me it was often a big struggle getting him to go to bed, and it usually required the assistance of sleeping aids. Their excitement was an indication to me that Reiki would be beneficial for Kyle and the rest of the family.

That evening, Mike and Deb agreed to let me conduct distant Reiki sessions on Kyle every other day for one year. To chart the effectiveness of the sessions and determine whether Kyle had a positive, negative or no reaction, we agreed I would check in with his mother for feedback.

DEBBIE

Two days later I began the Distant Reiki sessions. Distant Reiki occurs when the practitioner sets an intention to work on a specific recipient and, with permission, conducts the session as if the person were in the room with them, instead of at another location. It has the same benefits as performing Reiki in person. Energy, like a radio wave, is invisible and has no boundaries. But the transmission still occurs. Distant Reiki operates on the same principle. It is this same energy that drives our computer networks, powers the Internet, and links our smartphones. It is this web of energy that affirms that all life is interconnected.

I decided to conduct the sessions with Kyle before he went to school in the morning, just in case the Reiki energy was over-stimulating. After a few weeks of conducting these early morning sessions, I began receiving auditory messages that appeared to be in a child's voice. It was startling at first. I questioned myself, wondering whether I was so caught up in the process that my imagination had taken over. So many questions crossed my mind – how could this voice belong to a child who had never spoken aloud? But there also was a part of me that knew this was Kyle's inner voice, and it seemed as if he wanted me to share his messages with his family.

Once I was aware of the auditory messages, my attention and intention deepened. In the beginning, there were only a few words each session. But as the weeks progressed and I thought Kyle knew that I could actually *hear* him, the words began to sound more like poetry and prose. One morning, his words were so beautiful that I grabbed a pen and paper and wrote them down. That was the turning point—the communication was more meaningful than just symbolic. As time progressed and I became more comfortable in acknowledging to myself that it was Kyle *speaking to me* on an energetic level, I began to date and journal every message he gave me.

In the interim, I checked in with his mother to see whether there was any change in Kyle's behavior. I assured her that I had been faithful to conducting the scheduled sessions. Deb seemed grateful.

"Now that you mention it, Kyle seems less agitated and calmer," she said.

"Great," I replied. "I'm encouraged."

❧❧❧

After conducting the Distant Reiki sessions for six weeks, I asked Mike and Deb to meet me for lunch. I wanted to share with them what I had been learning. I brought along the journal and as I began reading what I had transcribed, both of Kyle's parents began to cry.

"This is Kyle speaking to us," his mother said.

Witnessing Mike and Deb's reactions made me realize that hearing the journal entries was akin to hearing their child's first words; a child who was nine years-old, but literally non-verbal. His mother took the journal and poured through the pages.

"There's no way you could've known about the Disney videos and those characters he adores watching, or how I have to open the supplements and blend them with his food because he won't swallow them," Deb said. She was very emotional when she exclaimed, "I had no idea that he loves to hear me sing!"

As I learned during that lunch, Kyle was sharing his thoughts and feelings about his daily life and routine – the small things that we adults had taken for granted, but were meaningful and noteworthy to him.

A few weeks later, while attending a workshop with other Reiki practitioners, I asked whether any of them had experienced anything similar to what was happening with me and

Kyle during the Distant Reiki sessions.

"Auditory messages aren't phenomena of Reiki," the workshop leader told me.

Once again, I felt both humbled and honored to have this ability, which had now become Kyle's vehicle to *speak* to his family.

At the suggestion of Mike and Deb, I purchased a voice-activated tape recorder to make it easier to gather notes from the sessions with Kyle. Initially, I was afraid that using the recorder would interrupt or stifle the flow of words I heard. Instead, the auditory messages came even faster and I was able to speak them aloud and record them on the spot. The more Kyle revealed his inner thoughts, feelings and hopes for the future, the more it became clear that beneath the mask of autism was a thinking, feeling little boy who experienced the same emotions, sensations, and daily challenges common to every child. Kyle once explained it this way: "We all have it in us; we just need to look deeper."

Regularly sharing my time and energy with Kyle and his family for five years without compensation was nothing compared to the gifts I received in return – hope, love, poetry and laughter, as well as a deeper understanding of the limitless capacity we all possess. Little did I know that this experience was preparing me for the journey I was to begin when I learned of Lauren Kiefer's death; a journey that has proven to be an often incomprehensible and amazing passageway illuminated by wisdom, courage and love.

10

Debbie

After watching five straight days of news broadcasts about Lauren's death, I knew at that point I was going to get involved. It seemed as if an invisible force was pushing me forward. Although I had only conducted a distant Reiki session from a photograph a few times, my experiences with my uncle, various clients, and conducting Distant Reiki sessions with Kyle convinced me that I might be able to tap into Lauren's life force and the energy of the evening of her death. I downloaded a photograph of Lauren from the Internet.

I sat quietly for several minutes looking at Lauren's picture before I felt and heard the connection. Visual images and words suddenly flooded my mind. I turned on my tape to record the descriptions of the images I was seeing and the messages I was receiving about the events that transpired Christmas night. I was surprised at how much information actually came through and how readily and easily it flowed. I heard two distinct voices – the murderer's and Lauren's – recounting the events of that horrific night. There was no doubt in my mind or my heart about what I was hearing. It's still upsetting to even recall the brutality of the scene I witnessed clairvoyantly and clairaudiently. I felt as if I were there in the midst of that horrifying experience and I was emotionally drained afterwards.

I recall, however, that when Lauren spoke, she seemed detached from the scene and the pain of it. She was definitely angry at the circumstances and angry at the perpetrator. But Lauren's main concern was for her mother. I thought she was an amazing daughter because of her expressions of gratitude that her mother wasn't there to also be hurt, and I recall thinking Lauren must've been a strong and mature young woman.

I truly believed Lauren was making the channeling session happen with such clarity. Her messages, recounted throughout this book as indented paragraphs written in italics, were loud and clear. She had something to say and nothing was going to stop her. The following is an excerpt from my transcribed notes, which I intuitively gathered and recorded on Dec. 31, 2006:

> *"The guy was shorter, slightly stocky. He appears to be about 5'7-5'10" tall. He had alcohol on his breath. He is wearing a dark jacket make of heavy cotton twill...maybe dark grey or black. He has dark brown hair, maybe in his late 20's, with a lighter complexion in contrast to his hair. He may drive a pick-up truck. He smokes. He is a jealous and possessive person. He has a conscience about his act... nervous...smoking a lot...pacing. I feel that he works in the trades. He speaks another language besides English."*

Although I was to eventually share all of the information I received that night with law enforcement authorities, I will not include any other details here because of the depravity and brutality of the crime.

After describing and showing what she went through, it became clear to me that Lauren was reaching out to her mother through me, but at the time I wasn't sure what to do about it. I heard her say:

"I am glad he didn't hurt my mom. She couldn't have taken it. How can someone be so cruel? How can he just take another person's life and just stomp on it? What will his family say when they find out?

"I am going to miss my mom but at least he didn't hurt her. I don't want her to cry anymore. He went crazy, insane, out of his mind...not thinking of the consequences."

I was exhausted and nervous when the session ended some 20 minutes later. I knew I had to make a decision whether to go to the police with the information I had just channeled, but I also wondered whether they would even believe me.

⟋⟍

Days later, the story of Lauren's death still dominated the news and everyone's conversation, especially since the perpetrator was still at large. While walking with Jeff along the Prairie Path on an unusually mild, January day, I shared with him a portion of the recording I had made during the channeling session with Lauren. Jeff was visibly upset that I had obtained what he believed to be invaluable information.

"You absolutely have to go to the police, Debbie," he said. "This information can help them break the case."

Although I couldn't be too sure that the authorities didn't already know what I had "seen" and "heard," I realized that the information could still be pertinent. I didn't make a commitment to Jeff, but I began working on my plan to contact the police. Unfortunately, I didn't get too much time to think about it. Jeff decided to contact the DuPage County Sheriff's Department on my behalf.

"I told them I had a psychic friend who had information to share regarding the Lauren Kiefer murder case," Jeff told me after he called them. "Don't worry. I didn't give them your name because I told them you were very reluctant to come forward. But I vouched for your character. They sound very interested to talk to you, Debbie, and I promised the detective I would encourage you to call.

"Here's the number," Jeff said, quickly reading it to me. "Please, call them, now, Debbie." He hung up before I could protest.

At first I was furious! I couldn't believe Jeff had called them and told them about me before I felt ready. As the events later unfolded, Jeff's call to the authorities was the push forward I needed. The next day, I reluctantly called the DuPage County Sheriff's homicide detective's number Jeff had given me, although I had no idea what to expect.

❧

The detective who answered the telephone seemed friendly. I started talking as soon as he finished telling me his name:

"My friend called you yesterday about me…about the Lauren Kiefer case," I said.

"Yes, ma'am," he replied.

"I want you to understand, I'm not a professional psychic and I'm not looking for any type of compensation."

"I understand, ma'am."

The next part felt like the hardest, but I took a deep breath and continued: "I have intuitively gathered details about the crime that I would like to share with you."

"I would like to hear more," he said right away. "I can meet you wherever you'd like to discuss it."

I didn't want anyone to know what I was doing and I certainly didn't want a law enforcement car pulling into my driveway. At the same time, I didn't want to just share what I knew over the telephone. I wanted to make sure that the authorities knew I was a credible person, not some crackpot, or someone seeking publicity. It would be better if he met me in person so that I could share a bit of background about myself before disclosing what I knew about the case. I took another deep breath.

"I'll come to the Sheriff's Department," I told the detective.

11

Debbie

The day I pulled my car into the parking lot of the DuPage County Government Complex for my appointment with the sheriff's homicide detectives had to be the coldest, dampest and most dreary day of January 2007.

I entered the stark county building only to find an intercom to announce myself and no place to sit down. On the wall was a poster-sized sketch of an eight year-old boy whose decomposed remains had been found on the side of a county road just before Thanksgiving. Looking at that poor child's sketch, which was most likely recreated based on the remains of his body, I imagined the terror he must have endured. The thought almost sent me running from the building. It took all the courage I had to stay focused and, while I waited, I constantly reminded myself I was doing the right thing.

The detective with whom I had spoken opened the door for me. His demeanor made me feel at ease and it gave me the strength to follow him. He led me into a small, plainly furnished conference room with harsh fluorescent lights and a table in the middle. Seated on one side of the table was a woman whom I assumed was also a detective.

"My name is Tiffany," she said standing to introduce herself. She shook my hand firmly.

"My name is Debbie," I responded.

"Have a seat," Tiffany said, motioning to the chair next to her. The other detective sat across the table from us.

I began talking as soon as I sat down, providing the detectives with my personal history. "I'm a former first grade teacher," I said nervously. "Now, I'm a real estate agent. I'm a mother, too. I've always been considered an intuitive, and about six years ago I began doing Reiki which is a Japanese…"

"I know about Reiki," Tiffany said, smiling.

I took a deep breath and relaxed when she said that. "Maybe she won't think I'm crazy," I thought to myself as I studied Tiffany's face. There was a kindness in her eyes; they were warm and welcoming.

"It was Reiki that helped me connect to additional intuitive gifts and the ability to channel…." Neither Tiffany nor the detective flinched when I said that.

"I only want one thing," I continued.

"What's that?" she asked.

"Anonymity," I responded. "I don't want anyone ever finding out, especially the perpetrator, that I had detailed information about the crime."

I didn't know the perpetrator's relationship to Lauren at the time, if any, and I didn't care to know. I was concerned about my safety, the safety of my daughter and my extended family.

"No one outside of the detectives will know anything about what you disclose," Tiffany said. "I promise."

On the basis of Tiffany's promise, I began to explain the process of channeling Lauren's energy. I pulled from my purse the transcribed notes from the session and began to read aloud from my notes of what Lauren shared with me. This is an edited excerpt:

> "…He spouted off nonsense…played games with my head…craziness. Picked up a weapon, swinging it like a crazy man…tapping it on the floor…anger in his heart. He was threatening. (But she was not thinking he would use it.) Where was his brain? What was he thinking? I don't want to talk about this anymore."

I had only read a few paragraphs when the male detective stopped me.

"Oh, no, what's going on?" I wondered, attempting to mask any traces of alarm on my face.

"Could you wait a minute while I call in another detective?" he asked. He returned shortly with another man.

"You can resume," Tiffany said.

I read for a few minutes when the new detective stopped me.

"We need to call in someone else," he said, looking at the other two detectives and not at me. He left the room and was gone for several minutes. When he returned, he was accompanied by a stern-looking gentleman, whom I could only assume was someone higher in authority. I looked at Tiffany. She nodded at me. I continued reading my notes. As I read my notes, I wondered if they thought I knew too much not to somehow be involved. I suddenly had second thoughts about being there. No one said a word until after I finished reading.

"Do you think you can get more?" the second detective asked.

"I…I don't know," I responded, surprised by the inquiry. "I'll try."

"Can you try now? Here, in this room?"

Tiffany offered me her voice recorder. Someone asked if having Lauren's personal belongings would help.

"I'm not sure. I've never done it using personal effects, or in an environment like this before."

The channeling I did at home using Lauren's photograph was emotional, but I was in no way prepared for the groundswell of feelings, images and sounds I experienced the moment I held Lauren's music CDs, jewelry, or looked at the family photos apparently taken Christmas Day. Seeing the pictures of Lauren's holiday celebration with her family and then knowing that her life ended just hours after those photos were taken was profoundly upsetting. I was grateful the detectives left me alone in that cold room. My hands shook as I pushed the button on the recorder.

Within a few minutes I was able to open the channel and receive the energy of Lauren's words. I think I was recording for 10, maybe 15 minutes; at least I thought I was. When I called the detectives back into the room I realized that in my anxiety, I had not pushed the record button. I called the detectives back into the room and shared whatever I could remember from the session, which was mostly a message to Lauren's mother telling her not to cry so much, and an acknowledgement that Lauren was worried about her. Lauren also talked about her grandfather and wondered how he was handling her death. She mentioned her sister, too.

"Lauren's mom told me she felt as if Lauren had been trying to contact her numerous times," Tiffany said.

I gave her a weak smile. I had become more emotionally involved than I could've ever imagined. I really wanted to go home, but I had not yet shared the "picture" of the perpetrator that Lauren had helped me see. I pulled out my notes again.

"Can you work with a sketch artist?" one of the detectives asked, interrupting the description.

"I'll give it a try."

It was surreal looking through all of the books of different facial features, like I had seen on television police shows. I worked with the sketch artist for what felt like an eternity but her drawing didn't fully capture the perpetrator's face.

"I'm done," I said suddenly. "I can't do this anymore. This is close enough."

I had been at the sheriff's office for more than five hours, and I was both physically and emotionally drained. The detectives had not verified any of the information I had given them about the night of the murder, and I did not ask if anything I told them was correct. I didn't need verification; I just wanted to help if I could. I know I could've chosen to ignore what I channeled and had less stress in my own life. But some unknown force seemed to be propelling me – I wasn't sure if it was the power of the universe or Lauren, but the pieces soon came to light.

"Thank you for coming in," Tiffany said, and then asked: "Can you continue to do the channeling?"

Without thinking, I nodded my head just so I could get out of there. Grabbing my coat and purse, I quickly left. Outside, it was dusk. The temperature had dipped and the cold dampness immediately set in, chilling me to the bone. I climbed into my car and burst into tears as I waited for the engine to warm up. I didn't even know Lauren or her family, but I was experiencing their incredible pain, sadness and agony. All I wanted to do was hold my own daughter close to me. The reality of the murder really hit me hard at that moment. It was probably seeing the pictures of Lauren's family and identifying with their loss. I again realized how tenuous life could be.

I called Erin to tell her what had happened. "I spoke with the detectives, honey," I said. "I'm all done."

"I'm so glad you did, Mom," she replied. 'I'm very proud of you."

"I love you and I'm so blessed to have you, Erin."

Being able to say that to my daughter meant more to me than I could ever express. Although I didn't personally know Lauren's mother, I not only knew, but could also feel how devastated she was because of the loss her daughter.

Part III

12

Janice

The detectives and district attorney occupied my house the week following Christmas, and during that time I was only able to pick up personal items if I was accompanied by a sheriff's escort. I could have never imagined when I left my home on Christmas to have dinner at Carli's that it would be the last day I lived in our house.

Police fingerprinted and questioned me, family members, and friends. They asked pointed and personal questions about our lives and collected personal belongings. One of the items collected was a check Lauren had written to her dad on Christmas for her car insurance. We were surprised when Tiffany pointed out that Lauren had dated the check Dec. 25, 1982, which was the year she was born.

The grueling investigation continued for a few months, but it seemed like a lifetime. It was hard dealing with the daily newspaper articles and nightly news broadcasts; constantly reading and hearing about what happened to my beautiful Lauren. I still could not believe that the death of the young woman everyone was talking about was my daughter. Watching our lives displayed and the evidence unfold on television was just like watching a horror film in which our lives were turned upside down in one split second.

Within a week of Lauren's death and in the midst of this traumatic time, my daughter began attempting to communicate with us. First, the lights began to flicker and light bulbs began to burn out. In some cases, the bulbs turned a dark yellow, spurted sparks and then burned out. Lamps blinked on and off and electronic equipment turned on and off. The lights where I worked also began blinking. We began to smell the scent of flowers when there were no flowers in the vicinity. I knew it was Lauren because I had read about the signs of After-death Communications (ADCs) in a magazine given to me by a friend. The magazine was published by Compassionate Friends, an organization for parents who've lost their children. The article, by Bill and Judy Guggenheim, authors of the book *Hello from Heaven*, noted 12 most frequent types of after-death communications parents report having with their deceased children. The list includes smelling a fragrance; feeling your deceased child's touch; or physical phenomena such as lights or lamps blinking on and off, electronic equipment being turned on and off, or objects suddenly moved.

This "communication" was happening at Carli's house and at mine where the detectives were camped out. I recall walking through my house with Tiffany, the district attorney, and Nick. While we were talking in my utility room – the room police believed the perpetrator used to gain entry to my house – the light in the ceiling dimmed very low, turned a dark yellow, sparked, and then burned out. We all looked at each other and we talked about it being a sign that Lauren was trying to tell us something.

An hour later, when I returned to Carli's she told me five

light bulbs had burned out in her house while I was away. I knew in my heart my sweet Lauren had so much to say and she was doing her best to communicate with us.

⚜

The phone rang in early February 2007. It was Tiffany.

"How are you doing, Janice?" she asked. Her voice was both thoughtful and compassionate.

"I'm not doing well," I cried. "I want my girl back."

I didn't know it at that time, but Tiffany's phone call that night would forever change my life. Even though her next words were shocking, yet believable and comforting, the conversation marked the beginning of a phenomenal journey and a turning point.

"Janice, someone has been talking to Lauren." Tiffany said.

"I don't need another kook in my life," I replied, listening with skepticism.

"Janice, would I set you up with a kook?"

I knew the answer to that question immediately. After all, Tiffany was a police detective. She didn't even have time for her own life, let alone time to seek out someone to help me. I trusted Tiffany unequivocally. She was so kind to me and my family. Tiffany went way above and beyond the call of duty by not just working diligently to solve the case, but also making time to call and check on how we were doing.

"We've met her, Janice," Tiffany assured me. "She's a successful business woman and a very kind person who wants to help because a friend of hers knew of Lauren. She also lost a child."

I continued talking to Tiffany as I ran to Carli's room repeating to her exactly what Tiffany was sharing with me: Lauren's beautiful message. At this point, I only recall a few words from that initial communication. Lauren talked about accompanying me on my walks, and she talked about her grandpa's scratchy whiskers. Lauren also gave this woman information about events only the two of us could have known.

Tiffany told me the woman had very specific and accurate details about Lauren's death, details she told Tiffany she received while channeling Lauren. The range of emotions I was feeling at that moment was indescribable.

"Can I meet this person and talk to Lauren myself?" I asked.

"No," Tiffany replied. "The woman wants to remain anonymous. I also want you to know that she's not seeking any compensation and she doesn't want anything from you or your family."

I began to anxiously await calls from Tiffany with messages from the kind woman communicating with Lauren, whose name I did not yet know. Without the gift of those messages, I would've never been able to carry on with my life, especially believing at the time that I'd never talk to Lauren again. My life would've been so different, in a terrible way. I was so grateful to everyone involved, especially to Tiffany and the kind woman who opened her heart to hear Lauren's pleas to help me.

13

Debbie

At Tiffany's request, I continued to "touch base" with Lauren when I intuitively felt I should do so. I also received signs to contact Lauren, such as flashes of thoughts about her when I wasn't consciously thinking of her, or I'd hear her name in my mind. Sometimes, I literally felt her presence.

Like I did when working with Kyle, I recorded every channeling session with Lauren and then transcribed the recording. Not only did Lauren communicate about the events surrounding her murder, she also expressed concern about the well-being of her family members.

Jan. 5, 2007:

"Everyone is crying. Everyone is upset. They haven't found him yet. He was evil. He was insecure. I didn't think he would do it. He crossed the line."

(Lauren indicated that she felt sorry for him, pitied him.)

As the channeling sessions continued, Lauren indicated that she wanted me to give her mother specific messages, and I emailed those messages to Tiffany. Because so much of the communication from Lauren was directed to her mother, Tiffany asked whether she could share the information with Lauren's mom.

"She feels as if her daughter is calling out to her," Tiffany told me. "It would help her so much if she were able to hear or read Lauren's words."

I agreed to send Tiffany two different transcripts – one for the police and the other specifically edited for Lauren's mom.

"But I don't want Lauren's mother to see or hear any of the details I share about the murder," I added. "I don't want her to relive that horror." I also made Tiffany promise not to disclose my identity. I just simply wanted to be the messenger and remain anonymous.

Over the next few months, I sent transcripts to Tiffany. I never asked for any details about the crime, and I never asked for validation of the information I shared about the perpetrator or the murder. I didn't want to be tainted by any clues. Regardless, I knew Tiffany couldn't tell me anything, so we didn't discuss it.

Tiffany did say Lauren's mother was grateful for the transcripts. Because the information was so detailed, Tiffany told me, Lauren's mother knew the messages were from her daughter, and they provided great comfort during an otherwise inconsolable time.

～◌～

Less than a month after her death, Lauren began to initiate more communication with me about her transition:

DEBBIE

Jan. 13, 2007:

"My Mom is still hurting. She's got to pick up the pieces and go on. There is silence in my voice. I have no place to be. I am just floating. Others are going to help me. Other souls take care of people like me."

(I'm getting the image of bridges…like they will take her across bridges. She is saying that there are patterns of godliness there. They are telling her she needs to come out of her Earth body. Patience…they are telling her patience…caring.)

"They are here to help me; here to take my soul somewhere. When I was little I wondered where I would go in death. I used to ask my mom where people go."

(She is saying that her grandpa will be mad that she is gone before him…he will say, "That it's not fair." The corners of his heart will be empty [without her]. He'll say, "Where is my little baby girl?" He could almost kill himself from the suffering and pain he is feeling over her loss. Her grandpa feels injustice. He feels cursed… that the family is cursed. I keep getting the image that her cheek is next to her grandpa's; that he sometimes had scratchy whiskers. But she loves him so much.)

"My heart wants to reach to them but I can't. Can you? Who are you? Are you someone I know? Are you a helper? Please tell my mom I love her; to please close the wounds in her heart. Tell her my secrets are always next to her."

(I perceive they had cute little secrets between them. She is saying that they [the secrets] will always still be.)

"Tell everyone to still be playful (she means within the family). Help their hearts empty the sadness. Pick up the pieces. Live your lives. Do this for me. Spend time thinking about me, but don't let it be horrible. Call on others to help you. It is okay to let family in to comfort. Spend your moments thinking about me, but try not to be sad. You are all in my heart forever."

"Life comes in funny packages. You get to be in it for a while, then the gift explodes. It is taken away from you by someone who is sad in their heart."

The next day, Lauren's comments seemed to be a tutorial for learning how to transcend. She wanted her mother to know what she was going through and that she was okay.

Jan. 14, 2007:

"They are preparing me. They say I will see my mom again."

(They are helping her transition.)

"They will take me to a place that will help me make decisions. To go to light; to a place where there are others like me. It's not scary. It just is what it is. I just need to learn some things about how all of this works. Those who care are here. They will help me. They will help me make choices. We all go through this, Mom, don't worry. It just

happened too soon to me. It wasn't my fault; it wasn't your fault, just sadness in someone's heart. A terrible uncontrolled rage. Possessiveness out of control."

During a channeling session with Lauren three days later, I began to get a sense of Lauren's sister. Lauren said her sister was tougher emotionally than she was:

"She has a spirit that won't quit. She has a good sense about other people. She'll help our mom through this. What is your role in this? Can you tell my mom all of this? How could he (the perpetrator) take life away from me?"

(She said he broke her, but not her spirit.)

"That can never be taken away. They (the helpers) are telling me that now."

I felt as if a shift had occurred in the dialogue with Lauren the next day. I remember feeling that her words were exceptionally poignant. I had a hard time even repeating them into the tape recorder. What Lauren said was so beautiful I cried as she shared it, and as I transcribed her words:

Jan. 18, 2007:

"I stopped floating, I feel better now. Those that are supposed to help me are helping. My Mom is still asking questions like 'Why did this all happen?' How could someone take her girl away? How can your children be stolen from you? Why does life suck?

"Who is this Tiffany woman? She likes my mom. Is she helping the police? She cries with my mom. She has a heart that's very deep and big.

"They (the helpers) are telling me that I was blessed with my family; I chose them to bring joy to their lives. It was someone else's anger that brought mine to an end. They need to try to pick up the pieces, to understand this horrible situation without guilt. In loving memory of me. In kisses on my head. Grandpa making jokes. Mommy laughing with Carli, spending time telling good stories.

"I know I am gone but I am with them. Knowing that evil does exist, but do not give up on the world. Love each other and hold each other. Smile when you think of me. Know that I am always available in your hearts...and to talk to.

"I hear your words, Mom. I hear your crying and your pleading. I can't come back, but I can be there in love, in your heart's wishes, that no one can take away from us. Be with Grandpa, he needs you.

"I know it was short, Mom, but other families don't have half of what we had. Look at this loser who did this. He didn't have enough love. He had sorrow. He had hurt and anger in his heart so big he had to hurt someone else to make his hurt go away. I had you all and I had your love. I could feel it every day. How many people have that? I was happy in my heart."

Ten days later, Tiffany emailed and asked me to check in with Lauren about the perpetrator. I felt as if I was bothering

Lauren because she previously had been so focused on communicating about her transition. Nonetheless, I obliged:

Jan. 28, 2007:

"I am more peaceful now. Things are sorting out here. Thank you for doing this for my mom. She worries about me."

(Lauren communicated that the police were looking for the perpetrator where they were supposed to. She said to look for the guy in "paths of least resistance." In an effort to get more specific details, I inquired again about the perpetrator.)

"He walks among you in plain sight. He thinks no one knows, but he knows. He can't do what he did and stay sane. 'Hey dude, we know you did it! What was in your heart that made you so angry? Conscience, you have a conscience. Tell them so this is over for my mom, so she can rest, so she can find some peace in her heart.'"

It would be weeks before I learned the real meaning of Lauren's messages about the perpetrator.

On Feb. 4, 2007, I woke up early and strongly felt Lauren's presence and that she might have something to say. Her beautiful message spoke volumes:

"I don't have revenge in my heart. I don't want my mom to have that. I promised her I would love her forever. You gave life to me, he took it away. Don't let resentment and anger govern your life. It is all about forgiveness and sor-

row for the life he had, not knowing how to control anger, wishing he had a better life than he did. I had a perfect life. His stupid act took it away. It is all about balancing these things in the world. Sending out love so others can understand. It is not about hate and turmoil, it is about honor and wishes for good for others. It's about picking up pieces, Mom, and moving on, keeping me in that place in your heart where you know you can always go to visit me and hug me and kiss me. I will feel it there (in her heart).

"I want you to feel it from me. I will always be present with you. I am not like I was, but in a different way. My soul is ascended to a place where others care for me and I can rest and reflect and say, 'Boy, was I a lucky girl' I had love in my family. I had joy in my heart. I had precious moments with you. Had time to kiss my grandpa…had plenty of friends and fun…you in my heart."

❦

I had been conducting the channeling sessions with Lauren for a little over a month but it felt like a year. I felt extremely stressed about the whole situation because I thought the police hadn't caught the murderer yet, and Lauren's picture still appeared on the news.

I was paranoid that the perpetrator would somehow find out what I was doing. I found myself searching for his vehicle, which Lauren had described to me, whenever I went to work out or to shop. I imagined he could be anywhere. Whenever I was home, I made sure the alarm system was turned on at all times.

Although my daughter, Erin, already knew, I finally told

my best friend, Linda, what I was doing because it was obvious how stressed I was. However, I didn't tell my parents because I didn't want to worry them. They would not understand why I was involved in what they would view as a risky situation. Despite the risks and fears, I continued channeling Lauren to assist with the police investigation. I just felt as if I was *supposed* to help.

14

Janice

Tiffany first read Lauren's beautiful words to me. Then she began to regularly email the transcripts to me. To hear Tiffany read the message was wonderful. But to actually hold my daughter's words in my hand was phenomenal.

> *"Believe in me, Mom; don't give up on life. I had beauty and you while I was there. I had sunshine every day. I had love all around me. Try to lift the heaviness out of your heart. It will not be good for you. I want you to smile again. Open your heart again. These are my wishes. Mom, I love you so much. Your heart breaking makes my heart break. I want you to hear this. I want this lady to let you hear this. People with closed hearts don't get to know this stuff. I am lucky for some reason this lady is doing this; giving this gift to you. She will get rewarded when she comes here. It's all about love and helping others and living the best life you can. It's not magic, it's just love. Look at the love I had. I was pretty smart too. I was a happy person. There aren't a lot of people who are happy. I had*

*happiness. I had happiness but it lasted a short time. I
had lots of love and kisses and wonderment in my life. You
have to dwell on that, Mom—that will get you through.
It (her life) was just all compressed. Kids wish for happy
lives when they're little and I got one. I had you for a mom.*

*"Please feel better. I want to see you smile. I want to see
that twinkling love in your eyes. I know it's there and it
will come back. You have to have hope. Don't let this ruin
your life. Please, Mom. Please try not to let it. Hey, I was
such a brat sometimes. Just think of that and smile. Don't
let the sun collapse, see it shining. Each day will get better.
Rainbows will come again. Holes will be filled in your
heart. Don't be depressed. Just feel better. Seek adventures
for you that won't involve sadness. Others will help you
through understanding and love, not hate or sorrow. Don't
let that consume you. You are too good for that, Mom.
Don't let the pain take over. Smile when you think of me.
Don't cry. Remember, I have a heart that's as big as the
universe. I got it from you. Our love is never-ending. It
will be in your soul when we meet again."*

Lauren's messages were personal, detailed and specific. Each
message reaffirmed that my daughter really was reaching out to
me. I felt so loved and cared for after reading Lauren's message.

But I also had so many mixed emotions. My daughter was
brutally murdered, and later I discovered she was reaching out
to communicate with me just days afterwards? It felt so hard to
comprehend. I missed her so much. But yet, she was sending
me a message letting me know that she was fine and how much
she loved me.

Maybe the mistake we make as human beings is to bury our

loved ones believing that we're leaving them at the gravesite. From the moment Lauren's messages showed she could still communicate with me, I started believing and responding to her as if she were still here. Hearing from Lauren helped me immensely during that time. I felt blessed that I could at least still have my beautiful daughter in this way.

～∂ᢙ

Shortly after Lauren passed away, a wonderful group of friends approached me and asked whether I wanted to organize an event in her honor. As I look back now, I wonder what my motivation was to do something so soon after her passing. But even though I was grieving, I felt my daughter deserved to have a day just for her, especially after what she had endured that Christmas.

My first thought was to organize a 5K run/walk in Lauren's honor because her daily fitness routine was so important to her. I wanted it to be a day that friends and family could celebrate the beautiful person she was, and to keep her memory alive. I also hoped the 5K would be the type of event that could replace the dreadful, detailed news reports about her tragic death with a positive story about Lauren's zest for life.

We decided the race would be held in June and formed a committee. My dear friends, co-workers and family were so giving of their time and energy. They took charge and immediately started making plans. With only six months until the race, we began working diligently to ensure Lauren's day would be perfect.

I'll never forget what happened at the first committee meeting. Carli and I arrived at the restaurant early to secure a table large enough for the group. I went to the ladies room. There, I asked Lauren: "Please show me that you're with us tonight." I was sure Lauren felt my need to have her with me. The feeling was always so strong, and I was so elated whenever she demonstrated her presence.

I walked back to the table where Carli was already seated. All at once, as if a fairy were waving her magic wand, the lights in the restaurant began to blink one by one. It was a chain reaction – a long row of lights across the bar area blinked first, followed by the lights in the restaurant area. It looked like a room filled with twinkling stars. Other customers in the restaurant watched Lauren's magical show in amazement. When it was over, they asked the wait staff what was going on. It was funny to see the staff shrug their shoulders and wave their hands in the air because they had no idea what had happened. Carli and I looked at each other and smiled.

"Thank you, Sweetheart, for being with us tonight," I said softly to Lauren.

Everyone talked across the table as we exchanged ideas for the 5K. When someone said we needed to create a logo for the event, I remembered that a friend of Lauren's had given me a metal angel figurine at her service. It just so happened that I still had the figurine in my coat pocket.

"Here's the logo." I said, taking out the angel to show everyone. The figurine had long hair and a body shape similar to Lauren's. Using the metal angel as the prototype, Lauren's Godfather, Steve, created the logo. He even used the shape of Lauren's cheek, which he took from one of her photographs, and superimposed it on to the angel's face. Our new logo had blonde hair and wore a blue dress with blue wings. We had to give her a special pair of shoes, of course, just like Lauren would've chosen for her outfit. We decided the angel would wear red high heels for formal correspondence, and would change into her athletic shoes for printed race materials.

As plans for the 5K became public, donations began pouring in – from our friends, neighbors, as well as from people who didn't know us. We received donations from people living in towns that weren't even remotely close to ours. Strangers sent condolences and prayers, along with their donations. Businesses generously committed to donating prizes for the raffle.

Lauren's most beautiful traits were her kindness and compassion toward others. We received countless emails and letters from people we'd never met telling us how kind Lauren was to them, or how she had helped them in some way. Given the type of person she was during her lifetime, Lauren left a positive legacy for us to continue with the 5K.

We decided to make the "Remembering Lauren 5K Run/Walk" an annual event, and we established the Lauren Kiefer Memorial Foundation, Inc., with all of the generous donations received. Not only would this event help keep Lauren's memory alive, the foundation would award scholarships to high school seniors who would be nominated based on their display of traits similar to Lauren's, such as an optimistic outlook, a zest for life, an effervescent personality, desire to help others, compassion, etc. The foundation was created and inspired by Lauren's love, and we knew she was still working very hard to bring people together for a positive purpose.

Of course, Lauren didn't just show up at our committee meeting to do magic and watch what was going on. She communicated her views on everything, which I received in the emails forwarded by Tiffany.

"I love the angel logo. I wear the gym shoes, but you do the running. I have wings on my feet now."

She also let me know that she had her hand in what was going on:

"But don't think you are doing it all on your own. I am orchestrating some of it. I handpicked the committee.

"It's a gift to them. It is a gracious understanding of loss turned into joy. My message is clear. Pain does not have to govern your life. You are the shining example of that. You are my hero, my love, my gratitude, my ever faithful gift.

"People will say, 'Wow, who's that Lauren?'"

15

Debbie

At the beginning of March, I called Tiffany.

"The stress has become unbearable," I told her. "Are you close to having a break in the case?"

By the tone of her response I was left with the impression that the police were close to solving the crime.

I burst into tears of relief, so happy at the mere prospect that the killer could be in custody. I was also relieved that I would hopefully no longer need to continue channeling for information. But Tiffany seemed to be reading my mind, and she had a different plan.

"Please ask Lauren if she can give you any more details about that night," she said to me.

Tiffany still hadn't confirmed any of the previous information I'd given her and now she was telling me the police still needed more. Despite my reservations, I was able to connect to Lauren. She shared additional details, but Lauren also communicated that she no longer wanted to talk about the day of her death:

"I have given you my say and now I am resting. Thank you for helping me."

I did continue reaching out to Lauren, but only if I felt the presence of her energy. Since she no longer wanted to talk about the perpetrator or the crime, my goal was to be available for her mother's sake. Tiffany said the messages from Lauren were keeping her mother going.

Mar. 22, 2007:

(I'm getting the sense that Lauren is farther away…not as accessible. She is more settled.)

"She (her mother) hears my prayers. My wish is for her to have peace with this horrible thing that happened. I have peace because I am here. It is harder to have it there. Those here have helped me. Here, time doesn't matter. There everyone is hurrying, swimming in their sorrows, wants and wishes. Can't they just appreciate life day to day…presents, gifts, and everyday things? Moments that are special?"

(The image Lauren is showing me is of her sitting on a couch cuddled next to a woman I believe is her mother. She is smiling. The other woman in the image is her sister, seated across the room teasing her, laughing a lot.)

"Being in those moments that you don't know will be taken away. Moments that my mom still has in her memory. In those joyous times. I want my mom to keep those moments present in her head, not the horror of what she saw,

and not the sorrow that is now in her heart, not the bitterness. Take away bitterness and hate and replace it with love. She has so much love in her heart I don't want her to hate. I don't want her to think of me and hate him. It will consume her. Try to erase the images. Dwell on my happy, cute baby face. Think about how I was such a little brat and laugh."

(I see her as a toddler running around and driving everyone crazy with her nonstop energy. I'm getting the sense that she was highly spirited and active.)

"I packed a lot into my short lifetime. I had more love than most people have, more fun and joy. Experiences, the best family I could ever have. Wishes, smart people who guided me. Lots of love and kisses. Opportunities. School. Shortened by a maniac who had hate in his heart."

(I'm getting the imagery of scissors in his brain, as if everything was cut up in his brain.)

"He will suffer now for what he did, because that is the payback. You can't do those things and get away with it. Mom, look at him and get rid of the image. Please don't keep it in your heart. Don't let hatred consume you. Let it all out again."

(I'm getting the sense that she is telling her mother to go and work out to help physically get rid of the pain.)

"It will help you. No one can carry that inside their heart and be healthy. You must try to let it go. I know I'd be

pissed as hell, too, but this is wisdom I can impart on you through all the gifts you have given me. Listen to your little girl who is not really a scatterbrain. I want you to move on and heal. Separate the evil from the goodness. Don't let hate consume you. It won't be good for you. It won't be good for your heart or your body. So many people carry hate in their hearts. I didn't have room for hate in my heart. I was taught by you to love. That is why I can pass this back to you, Mom. About love and forgiveness. Not acceptance for the act, but forgiveness for his heart that went awry because he didn't have the love that I did. He is to be pitied and scorned, yes, and punished for his act. Just let the police and the courts do the mechanics of it. Try to separate and know that justice will be done. It will help close a book in not thinking about him. Don't hold guilt, Mom. There is nothing you could have done that could have changed anything. It happened because of his hatred of himself. He is a battered soul. See light now, Mom, not darkness, fear or sorrow."

(She is saying that now she has time for contemplation, time to reflect and be grateful for all that she had. She is showing me an image of her cuddling with her mom and wants her to know that she is always next to her.)

"I know it's not the same, but I'm there. I know you feel me and you comfort me."

(I'm getting the sense that either her mom has a new hairdo or Lauren is playing with her mom's hair and telling her to get a new hairdo.)

"Mom, you are so cute. I want to see you joyous again. It's okay, Mom. It's okay to still laugh, still cry, but remember me and laugh. I want you to live your life with joy. I was taught by the best, you. Life's going to be tough for you, but you are a tough lady.

"It is a triumph for the police, tough for you, but it will hopefully make others think before they do an act.

"Carli will be there for you, Mom. She is tough. She knows how to hold things together. She is skilled at that."

Although I was looking forward to releasing the stress after the police caught the murderer, when Tiffany asked me to continue channeling I realized and accepted the fact that my relationship with Lauren and her family was not over. I wondered what my role would be. I had already sensed the shift in Lauren's focus away from the police to guiding her mother on the path to healing.

I was grateful to have been able to help the police and Lauren's family. I was learning so much from Lauren; her wisdom was profound. Mystically, I felt as if I were on an unchartered path. But I felt compelled to continue because it seemed clear that the time of higher purpose – healing – was now at hand. So, I continued to channel Lauren's energy whenever she summoned my attention.

16

Janice

The man who killed Lauren was tied to the murder by the DuPage County detectives with the help of the perpetrator's DNA collected at the crime scene. Not only did the perpetrator's genetic profile match Lauren's murder, it also matched the profile from a previously unsolved case in Aurora, Illinois.

State prosecutors announced the arrest during a news conference at the courthouse in March 2007, and they pledged that if the moratorium on the death penalty was lifted, it would be sought. I'll never forget how terrible that day was. It felt so surreal. I was so sure things like this didn't happen to people like us. Despite my best efforts to be a private person, we were now one of those unfortunate families for whom I'd always felt so bad whenever I saw their tragic stories of loss and grief on the news.

Later that afternoon, I was talking on the telephone to one of Lauren's friends. We were discussing the events of that day when I suddenly heard a loud banging on the back side of my house. I mentioned it to Lauren's friend and asked him to hold on while I ran outside to see what was going on. But there was nothing there. I put the incident out of mind until a friend came by that same evening. As we sat in the kitchen talking, the loud banging began again. We both ran outside to see what was happening. But there was no sign of anything suspicious. When we returned to the kitchen, the noise resumed. It sounded as if someone was banging on the outside siding of the house. But I still couldn't locate the source.

I decided to go work out after my friend left. I needed to release the tension and pent-up emotion I was feeling. I headed to the gym. It was late in the evening, and there was hardly anyone there. I went into the ladies room. Once again, I heard loud banging; it was on the door of the stall I was occupying. I ran out of the stall only to discover that I was alone. At that moment, I knew the banging I had been hearing all day was Lauren. She was expressing her feelings about the arrest. She knew what that day had been like for me and she was, as always, demonstrating her support.

✂⌒

The perpetrator spent nine months in the DuPage County jail while we awaited his trial. There were court hearings every three weeks during that time and Lauren's father attended every one. I could not attend the hearings and be in the same room with the man who took my daughter's life.

At the same time I was attempting to cope with losing Lauren, I was selling my home and trying to find a new place to live. I knew that vengeful thoughts about the man who murdered my daughter would not bring Lauren back. Instead, I sought to focus on the loving messages I was receiving from her. The heart-wrenching and thoughtful messages from Lauren that Tiffany forwarded via email carried me during that time. Despite the ordeal Lauren had endured, she still sent selfless, loving messages of care and concern about me and what I was going through:

"Mom hurt so much through this week. She'll never forget, but I hope she can forgive. I hope she finds a place of peace so it doesn't consume her every day. Have fun and experience joy. Be able to always smile when she thinks of me. I am with her in light… in the darkness of her room…in the specialness of our place, where we visit and hug and kiss and speak secret words. Where we find a special sense of peacefulness; time to reflect, and yes, to be sad, but to move on to a knowing place. Life isn't always great or perfect or on the timeline that you expect. It gets cuts short. It is about the dignity of dealing with it, about teaching others about the dignity. About scaling walls that you never thought you could; walking mountains, opening hearts.

"Live your dreams; smile your smiles. Don't let anyone or anything stop you because this happened. I know that your life will never be the same, but don't let it stop you from being who you are. Be brave, be honorable. Cry when you must. Call upon God to help you in your answers. He brought you to me through this woman, so you can hear me. To pick up the pieces and put them back into a collage of positivity and goodness and build upon that."

Lauren's messages were teaching me that love never dies; that our love was infinite, and it was growing stronger.

∽∂∾

Well-meaning friends suggested I see a doctor for medication to help me cope with the grief of Lauren's death. My doctor also asked whether I wanted a prescription for antidepressants because I was so sick over the loss of my daughter. Would a pill erase the vision of discovering the body of my brutally murdered child? Would a pill ease the pain of never being able to see her or hold her in my arms again?

As far as I was concerned, there was no pill that could ever take away the pain of losing my child; nothing could ease the symptoms of grief. The "easy fix" of taking pills was definitely not an option for me. People who suggested I take medication had no way of knowing what it felt like to be in my situation. Lauren heard them, and shortly after I received a message from her regarding the pills:

> "Sleep well, Mom. Don't take pills. Seek peace and clean ways for your body. Think of me with joy, not sorrow. Say I was a special girl who wasn't with you long, but shone every moment. She gave us joy and laughter. Even though she was taken away, she remains in our hearts where no one can take her away. She was a gift that we cherished, a special little Lauren. Even though she was a brat sometimes, she filled our hearts with sunshine, made all around us so happy. We will keep her in our hearts forever."

This message was incredible! The woman channeling and transcribing the messages from Lauren was a stranger. But my daughter's words were so familiar and a validation that she was *hearing* people talk to me. As a matter of fact, every subsequent message from Lauren brought me closer to the realization that there *is* life after death.

Although my daughter was not with me in body, she was with me in spirit. With every message, sound, and sign, I experienced it more and more. Because Lauren was able to send such beautiful and profound messages of wisdom, I knew my daughter certainly must be doing fine.

Lauren's messages helped me more than I could possibly express and reaffirmed for me that I did not need medication, nor did I need a grief counselor. Having contact with Lauren was the best possible "medicine" to get me through this difficult time.

Friends and family often said: "I don't know how you do it. I don't know how you get out of bed in the morning." They didn't know I had Lauren's help:

> *"You wait for my touch. I play a lot of tricks on you and you never know when they will happen. We are one. I help you get out of bed in the morning. It comes in waves. Sometimes I can touch you. Other times I can't. It's just the way it is. It's okay; it's not a constant stream. Just how it works; just how God works it. I want to continue to talk to you, but I don't know how long it will be. Just know that if it stops I am always in your heart. It's always there. No one can take the little dreams and secrets we had away. I know it's not fair, it just is."*

I only confided in some of our family and close friends about Lauren's messages, so it was understandable that others were puzzled.

Before Lauren's murder, I always felt if something happened to my girls, I would lay down, die and be buried next to them. But I learned that's not the way it works. Life goes on. The sun continues to rise and set. Still, I had to know and I continued to ask Laur, "How does life go on without you? Why did you have to leave me? How could this happen? How could you slip through my fingers, after I tried to take such good care of you?"

I beat my head against the wall trying to figure out the answers, repeatedly going over the scenario of that horrifying Christmas. I felt as if I was a failure as a mother. I should have been the one walking in on him that day, not Lauren. How could this happen to us after I prayed so hard for my daughters' safety and good health? Remaining in shock to this day, I still replay these questions in my mind. I still don't believe this really happened in our safe, small community – a place where my girls were raised and where we had lived for many years. I still don't believe this really happened in our own home.

⤜∞⤛

By March 2007, the entire situation had become more than we could handle. Thankfully, Carli and I were scheduled to visit relatives in Florida for our spring vacation. We just needed to get away from it all—the newspaper articles, TV coverage and people asking questions.

The day before we left, I received an email from Tiffany with a message from Lauren. I was elated! I read it over and over, analyzing and absorbing every word. The message was dated Mar. 22, 2007:

"To the whole family: Put me in your prayers. I can hear you all. Keep the feeling that I know you can hear me, and that I can hear you. The love doesn't stop; it keeps the channels of communication open in a different way, in a feeling way, not a talking way. In those moments when you think I'm near then concentrate and you will hear me love you and smell my body. Feel a tickle, hear a whisper, and know it's me. To let you know I love you and am at peace where I am at. Don't forget that, and don't be sad. Send kisses through the air and I will catch them."

The message from Lauren was an immeasurable gift.

Then, the most astonishing thing happened the next day. My dear friend, Joni, called and said she needed to see me. Even though I told Joni I was getting ready to leave for vacation and didn't have much time to visit, she was insistent.

"I really need to see you, Jan," she said. "I have something for you."

"Ok, Joni," I finally relented. "I'll take a few minutes to visit."

A little while later, Joni arrived bearing a gift. "I was in the store and I began to ask Lauren, 'What gift should I buy for your mom?'" Joni extended her hands and handed me a beautifully wrapped package.

I was astonished because I hadn't told Joni about the messages I was receiving from Lauren.

"I picked it up and put it down once," Joni explained as I opened the gift. "Then I found myself being led back to it again so I bought it."

"Oh my God!" I almost fell over with excitement.

"What? What?" Joni kept asking.

The gift was a lawn ornament with a cherub blowing a kiss The message I received from Lauren the previous day said to blow her kisses through the air and she would catch them. My precious Lauren had found a way, through Joni, to give me a gift that reinforced her message.

Joni said she felt compelled to see me and to bring over the present, even though it wasn't something she might have ordinarily purchased for me. I then confided to her the messages from Lauren, and we visited the entire afternoon. Time was no longer important that day, nothing else seemed to matter.

Today, the kissing cherub that Joni brought over the spring after Lauren's passing is located in a garden that I grow just for

Lauren—it's a beautiful flower garden to honor her. I plant many annuals and perennials. Growing in the midst of all of the pretty flowers, my Sweet Trixy (Lauren) added her personal touch – green onions. The onions return every spring. Lauren later relayed to me that the onions keep bugs out of the flowers. Actually, the onions are sometimes more fragrant than the flowers – my neighbor who lives two doors away says she can smell them.

∽◯◌∾

I felt a wave of emotions as we left for vacation the day after Joni gave me the cherub. I was deeply saddened because Lauren was not with us. But I was also happy because she had orchestrated the beautiful gift Joni delivered the day before.

The emotional roller coaster continued when I got to Florida. Although I had beach time to just sit and relax at the ocean, I constantly thought about Lauren and cried over the loss of my precious daughter. I was flooded with memories.

Lauren always sat on my lap, even when she was in her twenties. "Mom, am I too heavy?" she would always ask me.

"No, Laur, you're not," I replied, and I would squeeze her tightly, so she wouldn't move from my lap.

Sitting on the beach, missing and grieving my daughter, I suddenly felt pressure on my lap – it was just as if Lauren were sitting on me. "You are here with me, Sweetie," I thought to myself, and I was certain she was. I was grateful for the comfort she was constantly attempting to provide me.

More than once, I had experienced Lauren's efforts to let me know she was present. Just before leaving for vacation, I became conscious of feeling her touch and tickle. The sensation was most pronounced on my right temple, which I would later learn is one my strongest energy points. I also felt Lauren tickle and stroke my hair. At times, that sensation was so strong it actually felt like a mouse running through my hair, and I quickly touched it to make sure there was nothing there. Lauren also tickled my sister, her Aunt Jeanne, and we compared notes. It was the most wonderful, peaceful and uplifting feeling just knowing Lauren was with us.

After a few hours at the beach, we headed back to the house where we were staying. I climbed into the back seat of the car. On the drive to the house, I felt one pebble of sand – just one – moving in a zigzag motion up my arm and I knew Lauren was with me. The pebble scratched as it moved. I smiled as I looked down at my arm. There it was – one tiny pebble of sand.

I've never doubted that Lauren's messages, and signs, were genuine and truly coming from her. Because of Lauren's determination and love for me, I knew if anyone could communicate from the other side, Lauren would. I feel blessed to be able to communicate with my daughter after her passing. As time moves on, receiving these messages has become second nature to me.

17

Debbie

Nearly two months passed before I sensed Lauren's need for me to channel another message for her. From that communication, I could tell her experience was changing:

June 15, 2007:

(She is telling me that there is no concept of time for her where she is.)

"Memories come. I see them (her family) crying. I see them hugging each other. I am farther away now, but I can see them when I want to. I can walk among them. I can hear their hearts crying. They are getting a little better and I am glad. They shouldn't hurt like that. Moms shouldn't cry. Dads shouldn't grieve. They shouldn't say we miss her, because I am with them. They should open their eyes to sparkles in the light (because she is in the light). They will see my smile, feel feelings about me. I am always with them.

"I caress my mom in the quietness of her bedroom, in the early morning light when quietness surrounds the room. Feel me, Mom, know that I am there."

(She is showing me images of her Mom putting her arms out and hugging the air...knowing Lauren is there.)

"My mom needs you. You are my bridge. You can talk to her but it's not enough. She wants more. She is grieving. Reality is hard for her. She comprehends my loss, but in her heart she can't believe it. She doesn't want to believe it. It's too painful. Her little Lauren isn't there for her to hold and touch and squeeze.

"Mom, I love you. We will never be apart. All those special secrets...those that are only ours to play with and know that it's special. I will tickle you sometimes and you will know that it's me. Know that I live in the sunshine and that happiness can be yours. Don't feel guilty if you smile or laugh. Carli, too. My heart's heart. Don't feel guilty either. She is pretty special.

"When I was 'there' I would 'bust' you all (She said this in a humorous way). *I would also keep you all in line. Me, the brat, Lauren. I never gave anybody peace."*

(I perceived that she teased and was playful all of the time.)

"I want everyone to laugh, not to cry. Pick up your lives and smile when you think of me. Keep me in your hearts

forever and ever. I will play with you again."

(I see her rubbing her grandpa's head lovingly and kissing her grandma, I think, on the cheek.)

"You will all be fine. You have a lot of support. Look at all of the people who have helped you. Thanks for keeping my memory and love alive. We will sing together soon and never be apart."

One day while walking my dog, Sadie, in the park, I looked down and saw a sparkly rubber band used to hold a ponytail lying on the ground. I got a clear sense from seeing the sparkle of light that Lauren needed to communicate with me. Of course, I didn't have my tape recorder with me, so I made a mental note to visit with Lauren later. But when I got home, I forgot.

Later that day, I had an appointment to perform a Reiki session. When I walked into the main office, I saw an 8x10-inch photograph of Lauren on the desk, advertising the 5K in her honor. I smiled.

"Lauren, I'm sorry I forgot to contact you," I thought to myself, "I will visit you tonight."

The photo had a dual meaning. Besides reminding me to check in with Lauren, it also reminded me of the recent conversation I had with Tiffany. She mentioned the 5K and asked whether I wanted to attend with her. I was reluctant. If I went, I knew I'd have to reveal myself to Lauren's mom. Now, I understood the purpose of Lauren's contact – *she* wanted me to go.

On the day of the 5K, June 23, 2007, the dark clouds threatened rain. It took all of the courage I could muster to honor my commitment to meet Tiffany and her mother at the high school athletic field. Despite my reservations and feeling anxious about what might happen, I knew I had to be there. Over the past six months, Tiffany had shown tremendous compassion and patience. Not only did she deliver the messages I channeled from Lauren, she tirelessly worked on the murder investigation. I couldn't believe how she went above and beyond the call of duty. Her immense dedication helped in countless ways. I couldn't let her down.

I learned from Tiffany that sharing the messages with Lauren's mother had been helpful, but I also wondered whether meeting me in person might be too difficult – especially on this day organized to celebrate and honor Lauren's life. As I walked across the athletic field through the crowd of runners and walkers in search of Tiffany, I suddenly had a recollection: I recalled seeing Lauren's father during a television news report the day authorities charged the perpetrator with Lauren's murder. Her father's first name was Nick. Although I didn't recognize him at the time, I remembered a guy in high school whose name was Nick Kiefer. I always meant to ask Tiffany if she knew where Lauren's father went to school, but I never did. Now, I wondered whether he could possibly be Lauren's father. And hadn't I heard that Nick Kiefer married a girl named Jan? Could his wife possibly be a girl named Janice with whom I occasionally talked between classes in the high school hall, and who I recalled dated Nick? Did this mean I was already acquainted with Lauren's parents, even though I hadn't seen them since high school?

My questions were soon answered. Tiffany then walked up to me and asked, "Are you ready to meet Lauren's mom?" I took a deep breath and began walking with Tiffany towards a woman with red hair.

"Debbie Smania?" Jan said, calling me by my maiden name before Tiffany could introduce us. It was unbelievable – Janice Lopardo, one of the popular girls in high school, was Lauren's mom. Jan and I hugged and cried in disbelief and recognition that it was Lauren who had brought us back together.

18

Janice

The first "Remembering Lauren 5K Run/Walk" began at the high school and looped through the town of Villa Park, Illinois. More than 1,000 runners and walkers, and 250 volunteers participated in the event despite pouring rain and the unseasonably cool temperature. I was so overwhelmed to see all the people who'd come out in tribute to my daughter's life. The high school football field was swarming with people from our community and surrounding areas. I always knew Lauren was and is special, but this outpouring of support confirmed it.

It was quite an event – vendors, live entertainment and raffle prizes. The most important part of the day for me was the tribute to Lauren, which was held in front of an oversized canvas photograph of her. Carli was in charge of the entertainment and chose the song "Fix You" by Cold Play, one of Lauren's favorite groups. The participants gathered around Lauren's photo, their hearts filled with love. On the count of three everyone shouted "Hollar!" which was Lauren's favorite greeting. Then, 500 red balloons were released while the band sang. We were speechless. It was so quiet and the crowd was so solemn. There were so many tears as we watched the red balloons float towards the heavens. It was such a sad moment – all of us aware that Lauren was gone and never coming home.

In the midst of the 500 red balloons, we suddenly noticed one blue balloon pushing its way past the others racing to the top of the bunch. Many of the spectators noticed the blue balloon. I even received calls asking about the source of the blue balloon. I had no idea, so I checked with the volunteers involved with the balloon launch. But no one saw a blue one when they were filling the balloons with helium. In the days following the race, a blue balloon would pop out of nowhere in the oddest of places.

The foundation was able to raise enough funds at this first event to make it possible for us to carry on Lauren's spirit to help families in need. We also awarded scholarships to high school seniors and donated money to several non-profit organizations.

◌◌◌

In the midst of all the activities and preparations for the first run, I saw Tiffany walking towards me. She was accompanied by a tall, beautiful blonde woman who looked familiar. I recalled Tiffany saying the woman communicating with Lauren might attend the race, and I wondered if this could be her. Suddenly, the woman's identity dawned on me. I knew her from high school.

"Debbie Smania?" I said. We hugged and cried. I was in awe that it was Debbie standing before me and that she was actually the person communicating with my daughter. At that moment, I lost sight of everything going on around me. I just wanted to talk to Debbie; to ask her questions, and thank her for all she had done. But it wasn't the time or place to talk.

However, I was so grateful that both she and Tiffany attended the event. I hugged Debbie tightly again and thanked her for helping to reunite me with my daughter.

19

Debbie

Tiffany forwarded to me a thank you letter from Jan a few days after the 5K. I was grateful she didn't ask me to call her, and I was relieved she didn't ask for a meeting because I wasn't yet sure how I felt about what role, if any, I might have in her life. All along, my main concern about finally meeting Lauren's mother was that she might want to see me too often; she might not want to continue the healing process on her own. I already questioned whether I had interfered too much in Jan's life. I decided I would only forward messages on to Jan if Lauren contacted me.

A month after the 5K, Lauren did let me know that she wanted to communicate with her mother, and I transcribed the channeling session and forwarded it to Tiffany:

July 22, 2007:

"I am more peaceful now; the (5K) run helped. Everyone supporting Mom; everyone remembering me; everyone

missing me, even people I didn't know. They were there to share love, to be filled with grief, but letting it go. In their hearts saying, it happened, but we need to move on. Picking up pieces and putting them back together like a puzzle. Putting me in their special places in their hearts."

(She shows me images of some of her former employers who attended the 5K.)

"I had so much fun in life. I like the picture you picked of me (for the race). I looked pretty cute, didn't I? Thumbs up!

"It is so hard to understand the anger in someone's heart. How could he do such a thing? He is being punished. He didn't have any love, didn't have the family I have. His heart was crushed. He wanted to make someone else hurt, too. He sits now in a prison. Behind bars where he can't hurt anyone else, to be judged, to be found to have a disturbed nature, a cold, calculating, twisted brain. Normal people can't even imagine. He was raging; he is spineless. He got mad that I defended myself. I said, 'What the hell are you doing here?' I said, 'I don't want you around me.'

"The coroner needs to look further. He came to hurt me, not to rob the house. He made it look that way. It was Christmas and he had no one. He was jealous. He had no love; didn't feel like he belonged. Is he going to be killed?"

(She shows me that she wants him to get help and to be locked up; she doesn't want him harmed.)

DEBBIE

"Tell Mom I love her. I love her big smile, our good times. It will get better each day. I will love you always. Have no fear of that. I am your baby girl in my little sweet way. Put me in your pocket and keep me there. I will stay and make you smile. I will tickle you sometimes so you know I am there. I love to make you laugh. You are my mom, my friend, the one I love the most."

20

Janice

I received a call from a friend inviting me to go with her and her family to visit a medium. I know the Bible frowns upon talking to a medium. However, I felt I had been dealt an awful hand, and I needed to get through this situation whatever way possible. I truly believed that God, Himself, had given me this gift. He brought me and Debbie together. But I wanted more contact with Lauren.

I was sure any parent in my situation would want ongoing contact if their child suddenly had been taken from them. I knew I wasn't supposed to directly contact Debbie, but I thought, if I could find her number on one of the emails and talk to her, she might be willing to see me.

I began thinking about Lauren and communicating with her in my mind to find out whether I should see a medium. I didn't know what to do. I wanted so badly to talk to Lauren, but only trusted Debbie. I wrote the question on a piece of paper and I immediately felt tickling throughout my hair. I knew Lauren's answer was to contact someone.

Out of desperation, I went to my computer and pulled up

all the emails from Tiffany. Somewhere, I was certain there'd be information about how to contact Debbie. I began searching through the email, even though Tiffany said I wasn't supposed to contact Debbie. But now I needed her insight. I wasn't concerned whether Debbie would be angry with me for calling her. Besides, I also wanted to personally thank her again for sending the messages from Lauren.

I found Debbie's telephone number – information I was sure she left in an email accidentally – and I called her. When she answered the telephone, Debbie's voice was so warm and welcoming. I instinctively trusted her because she had selflessly become close to Lauren.

After apologizing for violating her request that I not directly contact her, and thanking her for all of her help, I explained my situation: "My friend asked whether I wanted to see a medium and I received a sign from Lauren that she wanted me to go. But, you've been my trusted contact with Lauren. To be honest, I don't want to see anyone else."

Debbie and I talked for two hours, and I knew I was making the right decision. We exchanged stories about our contacts with Lauren. At the end of our conversation, we agreed to get together for dinner.

About a week later, we met for dinner. "Do you think I might be able to have a channeling session with you?" I asked at the end of our four-hour dinner. Debbie agreed to see me, and I was so grateful.

୬୦ଙ

I don't recall all the details of that first session I had with Debbie. I just remember being really nervous going to the facility where Debbie practiced. I brought along a bag containing some of Lauren's things, thinking that Lauren might talk to me if her things were in the room. But I quickly found out from Debbie, they were unnecessary.

We didn't tape that session. The next day, I wrote down what I could remember from my exchange with Lauren:

"What she gives us is a gift. It's a horrible thing that happened. But there is nothing you could have done about it, so don't keep going over it in your head. Let this woman do her job. I want you to move on and be happy; I don't want you to cry anymore. I am with you in love, caring and sharing. We are blessed with a gift that not everyone gets, and I get it from our love and being opened to it. We are so lucky."

"I miss you so much, Laur," I said. Then I asked her whether she enjoyed the 5K in her honor.

"The balloon launch was cool."

"Did you bring the blue balloon, honey?"

"I can't answer that. I looked so cute in the picture.

"You looked as beautiful as always, sweetheart."

Lauren also communicated that she wanted me to do good for people; continue her efforts where she left off.

"Listen to suggestions that come into your ear."

Debbie and I talked about getting together again. Just thinking about that day, I realize now how upset I was during the first session. But over the years, Lauren has helped me understand our collective mission:

"I counted on you, and now you count on me. Two peas in a pod. Two angels with wings. Two winners in our own way. Building scaffolding to the sky. Our triumphs will be heard by all. Songs will be heralded. People will applaud your courage to share with others my wishes. Your knowing to do this. Driving past your fears to share. To show my life was not a waste. It was a message from God. I am the receiver, you are the deliverer. I am in the corners of your heart, in ways to support you, to follow you wherever you go. My hand is with yours. Our hearts are intertwined. Our noses are touching. Our feet in golden shoes. My dance is your music. My wings support you. I pay tribute to you. I'm small, but you have made me large. Like a bird singing for others to touch their hearts. For others to know me, that didn't know me."

Looking back now, I realize how Lauren has guided me along the way, and I can see how my daughter and I have united together from our different places.

21

Debbie

The moment I heard Jan's voice on my cell phone, I knew I must've sent an email to Tiffany with a message from Lauren, and my telephone number slipped through. Although I had wanted to keep my distance, that day Jan and I must've talked for two hours. It was clear we had a lot of catching up to do since we had not seen each other since high school, and it felt right.

I agreed to see Jan as a client and conduct a channeling session with Lauren for her. As I was to learn, it was a benefit for both of us. Jan began to visit my practice every few months. Lauren's energy often showed up and the sessions were always emotional. Jan and I laughed and cried together in response to what Lauren communicated.

After a few sessions, Jan asked if she could record them. Although I don't normally allow my clients to do so, I knew Lauren's messages were very important to Jan. The reason I don't allow clients to tape the session is that it distracts from their being focused on the present moment of what they're hearing and feeling. However, during the sessions with Jan and Lauren, I realized quickly that recording them was imperative.

The messages were both poignant and lengthy, and we both knew we'd never be able to remember everything Lauren said. Besides, what Lauren was sharing was too important to miss a word. Jan brought a tape recorder with her to our subsequent sessions, and she then transcribed the recordings.

22

Janice

I lost Nani less than a year after Lauren passed, in October 2007. Baba died in April 2008. They were both very ill and eighty-three years old. Losing their precious granddaughter, who was only 24-years-old, took an enormous toll on them. It was an even greater pain than their illness.

In November 2007, Lauren asked during a channeling session:

"Is Baba coming here soon? He will be happier when he gets here. He will be with his family when he gets here. Tell my grandpa, I love him. My grandma is not ready to speak yet."

"Will you meet him when he gets there, Laurie?" I asked her.

"The angels will help him with his transition, just like they helped me, and he will have peace. Let him go peacefully."

During the time I was receiving Lauren's messages, my dad was receiving chemotherapy. As he rested at home in a hospital bed, he sometimes would sing a song in his sleep. He always sang the same song and it was beautiful. Jeanne and I sat next to him attempting to interpret the words. But we couldn't understand what he was singing. At the end of the song, our father whistled and smiled. This continued for a few months before he passed. It was really peaceful to see him this way, especially after he'd been ill for such a long time.

Baba told me that he saw Lauren often.

"How does she look, Dad?" I asked him.

"The same – really busy and moving all the time, just like she always was here," he said.

I can still see Baba sitting in his chair reading the first channeled message I received from Lauren. Tears streamed down his cheeks. Although his heart was broken, Lauren's message helped him, too, because he also was certain it was her speaking. I was so happy to be able to bring him some sort of comfort with that message before he passed on.

We buried three family members within 17 months: Lauren, Nani and Baba. The heartache and loss was really too much for one family to endure. Lauren was very close to her grandparents, especially her Baba, and from what she told me during one channeling session, they still were:

"Baba had a hard time with his transition because of what happened to me, but he's better now. Baba is still making jokes and doesn't have to shave here. He is with his friends, and making everyone laugh. Baba is playing cards; he makes friends easy. Nani is at peace. She can't believe all the tricks I play on you.

JANICE

"Nani and Baba were ready to come here. They are home."

During a channeling session nearly two years later, on Aug. 13, 2009, I asked Lauren how she was doing.

"Baba is watching me. He has arms that are strong, love that is pure, whiskers that still scratch, wisdom in his heart, patience in his soul, comfort in his words. He keeps me grounded from being too sad."

My father then communicated with me using Debbie as the channel:

"You knew before anything happened to Lauren, you had it in your heart that something would happen to her. Counterintuitive. It was her destiny. We're together in spirit, we'll be together again. No pain honey, only love. No medicine, no chemo, no junk being put into my body. Now I'm okay. I love you.

"Be gentle on yourself, Lauren is proud of you. She gives you gifts. She's pretty active. She's a fireball, no one can keep her down. She's writing this book.

"She's dynamic. She'll help you by doing this. Make sure you mention Jeanne, and of course, tell them how handsome I am.

This was my dad speaking. His words were so familiar and he was always joking when he was here. I was amazed. It was such an emotional session. I felt so blessed, receiving my father's advice and comfort once again. It was as if he hugged me and told me everything would be fine, just as he always did. He still had the same humorous personality as he did on earth. I was crying and laughing simultaneously, and saying out loud, "That's my father!"

I told him how I missed his cute, fat cheeks, and his reply was:

"Handsome devil, with two beautiful daughters. Is Jeanne okay?"

"No we're not okay, we miss and love you people!"

"Just do your work until you're with us. Tell Jeanne that, too. We love you and your wisdom. Nani is quiet and at peace. Pick yourself up and move your life forward. I like your direction. I like how you are expressing your feelings."

Those messages were very important to me because it re-affirmed that my family was reunited in heaven, just as we're promised, and they were healed. The message from Baba also reaffirmed that my premonitions about losing Lauren were accurate. But most important, I was very grateful they were all at peace and happy together again. Lauren reminded me that I was never alone, and I'm very grateful and felt extremely blessed to know that Lauren is always nearby, whenever I need her:

"Whether you know it or not, I'm always there. Sounds on the carpet. Whispers in your hair. I smile on a lot of people. I know when to make my presence known. My destiny is your sorrow, a calling upon your inner strength. Mom, I know you can do it cause you're strong. Better times ahead.

I'm a pretty smart kid, huh? One who is wise beyond her years. A petal in your flower box."

"You are my rose, Laurie."

"Signals from me to let you know I'm okay. I drop in unexpectedly. No invitation."

"I love when you're here. You don't need an invitation."

"It's so different where I am. No way to explain it. It's not about missing when I'm here. It's about the loving when I was there. Mom, are you stumped by all of this?"

23

Janice

The week of Christmas 2007 the perpetrator committed suicide in the DuPage County Jail. He took an overdose of the medication he had been saving. It was a senseless crime and my daughter was an innocent victim of his self-hatred.

The night the perpetrator took his life, I was at my health club talking with some friends. The Christmas lights strung across the mirror began blinking off and on with a vengeance, and half of the basketball court's lighting went out. I wondered whether we were having a power outage. At the same time, I questioned whether it was Lauren. Just as quickly, I said to myself: "You can't always think it's Lauren, even though she has used flashing lights before to communicate."

The next day Tiffany called me at work and said she had some news. "Can I come to your office to speak with you?" she asked.

"Why? What happened?" I responded.

"It's important. I prefer to speak with you in person."

I immediately emailed Carli to tell her that Tiffany was coming over with some news for us. Carli wrote back immediately: "Maybe he killed himself."

I anxiously waited for Tiffany to arrive. I couldn't imagine what was so important that she needed to see me in person. She arrived less than an hour later.

"Is there somewhere we can talk privately?" Tiffany asked.

I escorted her into an empty office. "What's going on?" I was anxious and on edge.

"He's dead." Tiffany responded.

I could hardly believe my ears. "He's dead?" I repeated.

Tiffany told me the perpetrator committed suicide in his cell. As it turned out, the time of his death was the exact time the lights began flashing at the health club. The flashing lights *were a message from Lauren.*

The next day, a friend who also believes in the authenticity of the messages from Lauren, came into my office at work. "Jan, Lauren was telling us that he took his life last night," she said. "Every light in my house was blinking at that time."

∽ゝ∂⌣

After Lauren's death, Christmas became the most difficult time of the year for our family. It wasn't just the day. It was the entire season of celebration, which began in November and ended in January. While everyone else was merry, shopping, and attending parties, I found myself depressed, filled with dread, and wanting the holidays to just end. We were all missing our girl, and everything felt so unreal.

Celebrating Christmas Eve, which had been our family's favorite holiday tradition, was now just another day we had to learn to manage. We no longer had a party at our house. After visiting Lauren at the cemetery, our family gathered at a restaurant. On Christmas, we had dinner at Carli's house but it wasn't like the Christmases when our Lauren was with us. I tried to stay strong for Carli and she tried to be strong for me. But I was so out of sorts on that day, quietly reliving every horrible moment of Christmas Day 2006.

During the Christmas evening hours, the hours that were the most unbearable, we attended a vigil for Lauren hosted by her adoring friends. We shared funny stories about Lauren, played her music, and watched a slide presentation of photos and treasured memories. Spending time with Lauren's friends was comforting because we all had the same feeling of loss. Unfortunately, as the years have passed our feelings of loss haven't lessened.

⋘◦⋙

One Friday afternoon, I reluctantly walked into my spare bedroom, a room I hardly entered, with the plan to clean it. There were some papers and photographs I kept in there that I decided I needed to sort through. A few minutes into cleaning, I discovered a greeting card Lauren had written to her close friend, Julie. Julie had been living out of town for a while, and Lauren must have forgotten to mail this card to her.

The card read as if Lauren were writing Julie now. Lauren wrote:

> *"This summer flew by and I always get sad at this time. Even though I didn't see you that much I still love you, my 'bestest friend.'"*

I was only in the room for 10 minutes, but after finding the card I felt as if I had finished cleaning. I left it lying on the bed so that I would remember to give it to Julie the next time I saw her. I soon realized the *real* purpose for "cleaning" that room.

When I returned to work Monday, I learned from a mutual friend that Julie's father had become gravely ill over the weekend and almost died. The next morning when I woke up, I happened to look across the hall in to my spare bedroom. The card lying on the bed caught my attention. Although the room was very dark, the flowers on the front of the card looked as if they were three-dimensional and outlined in silver.

"Oh my God, Lauren," I said aloud. "You had me find that card so I could give it to Julie in her time of need." I literally could not breathe at that moment. What a miracle!

I called Julie that day. She was so delighted to receive the message from Lauren.

"I knew Lauren was with my dad because he's going to be fine" Julie said.

That day, Lauren taught me the meaning of the phrase, "You take my breath away."

During a later channeling session, Lauren explained to me the genesis of her mission:

"The truth cannot be shadowed. I developed a rapport with God. He touched my spirit when I was young. He drew me into His knowing. I called upon angels. They brought me to a place of peace. Others need to know they can do that. They came early in my life. Showed me God. Awakened my spirit. Talked of ethereal things. Soothed my worries. Made it easy for me to tell others about God.

"Secrets unfolded to me when I was young. I was touched in a special way by God. I knew I was different."

"Why didn't you tell me?" I asked Lauren.

"How could I explain such a thing? Why do think I ran so fast? I had to get it all in. A busy bee."

24

Janice

Debbie and I were planning to schedule a channeling session to connect with Lauren on her birthday. I desperately wanted to communicate with Lauren on that day. Lauren overheard our conversation and before we could complete our plans, she contacted Debbie. It was the week before her birthday in February 2008. She had a message for me:

"Tell my mom I want to give her a gift for my birthday. Tell her that I am never lonely here, that there is always someone with me. Tell her that I want her to be happy. Tell her that grieving me will only bring her sadness and that she is an amazing woman. She opens others' hearts because hers has been opened. She inspires others because of her positive attitude and how she is living her life. She never makes them feel uncomfortable about me. Mom wishes that others would let her go on and stop asking how she is doing. She would just like to be free of the labels; of others snooping in her business and feeling sorry for her, or wondering how she's doing. SHE IS FINE! SHE IS MY

MOM! What do you expect? She is fine. She is beautiful"

The fact that Lauren contacted Debbie before we could confirm our plans left me speechless. Lauren reminded me she overheard all our conversations. You can imagine the happiness this message brought me.

While friends and family had been very supportive, like Lauren said in her message, I was ready for people to stop feeling sorry for me. I was tired of the label, "the poor woman whose daughter was murdered." I wanted to grieve my daughter in my own personal way and not publicly.

I still met with Debbie for the channeling session on what would've been Lauren's 26th birthday, Feb. 25, 2008. It was a very emotional time for all of us. "Happy Birthday, Honey" I said, as soon as Debbie let me know that Lauren was present with us.

Lauren requested that Debbie and I sing the "Happy Birthday" song to her. Our hearts were broken at that moment and Debbie and I cried as we sang, "Happy birthday to you, sweet Lauren." After we sang, she spoke to me through Debbie:

"I know, Mom, it's terrible. But we have each other in different ways. I see your heart broken, Mom, but repairing like a puzzle. It won't always be that way."

"Why did you have to leave me"? I asked.

"That is the way it was supposed to be. It is out of our control. My heart beats in your heart, Mom."

"I know Laur." I replied. "I feel it beating inside of mine."

I *could* actually feel Lauren's heart beating at that very moment, which was more emotionally intense than I could've ever imagined.

"We have a gift; it's like in a big box. It's better than a pair of three-inch heels. I hope you know that I was a package, like a gift, and I wasn't supposed to last until I'm old."

"You're a gift, Laur, which I thank God for. I still have your pair of silver, three-inch heels, which I know were one of your favorites."

"Get rid of those already. Are you going to wear them?"

"No, I just kiss them."

"Remember, Mom, how you used to kiss my feet? Only a mother would do that. My hand is always on yours. I am always with you, even if I can't give you a sign. Sometimes it's hard to get through the energy. Our hearts are together, like in a cradle. Say I love you again, I love hearing it."

"I love you, Sweetheart."

"I love you, Mom. Coincidences are few. If you think it's me, it probably is. I have ways I like to make you laugh. Your tears need to happen, but not as often. Collect my thoughts and keep them in your head. Don't destroy yourself with your grief. Present a conscious role model to others. Select those who do not make you feel comfortable, kick them out. Learn from them but don't dwell with them. Promise me you'll always love me."

"Oh Laur, I will love you forever, Infinity."

Lauren always mentioned something during the channeling sessions that only the two of us knew. During that session, Lauren shared how much we loved each other, and how that closeness was demonstrated by my love of her feet. She reminded me how I kissed and tickled her feet all the time. Those types of reminders were constant reaffirmations that the communications Debbie channeled were really from my daughter.

❧

Debbie called me on a Friday morning saying that she was in the park with Sadie, and a bird was staring at her.

"I'm not calling Lauren a bird," she said. "But it was Lauren and she said:

"Tell my mom to invest her money wisely."

That was no earth-shattering message. But the fact that Jeanne and I had an appointment at the bank that afternoon to settle our dad's estate, well, I almost fell off my chair, especially since Debbie had no idea I was going to the bank that day. I'm sure my dad was prompting Lauren to give me the message. When he was here on earth, he never wanted us to go shopping or spend too much money.

❧

On Mother's Day weekend 2008, I was at the movie theater, and fell asleep while watching a film. I awoke abruptly and saw two hands holding a necklace. The chain was stretched in front of me as if it were going to be placed around my neck. I instantly thought of Lauren's hands when she placed the necklace around my neck on our last Christmas Eve together.

When I returned home from the show that evening, I actually felt Lauren sitting on my bed. She was saying, "Happy Mother's Day, Mom." How remarkable that she wanted me to know that she still celebrated holidays with me.

Lauren also was still pulling pranks. She enjoyed turning my television off and on, turning my lights on and off, and my computer off when it was on. I remember one time walking up the stairs with the charger to my computer in my hands, only to discover that my computer's blue power light was already illuminated. Lauren even illuminated light bulbs when the power was turned off.

∽ე ᕲᕽ

Susan and I worked together for eight years. When Lauren was murdered, she was among the first to come to my office to express her heartfelt sympathy. We've since become close friends. She's been there for me, not only as a friend and moral supporter, but as an important member of the Lauren Kiefer Memorial Foundation.

Susan knew what I was going through because she had lost her sister some years before. So it seemed only natural to me that Susan would be the person I confided in when I began receiving the transcripts of Lauren's messages. We cried together, sometimes in the oddest of public places, while talking about Lauren's amazing messages and what we were learning from her. Susan also received several visitations from Lauren through vivid dreams. Lauren was thanking her for her role in the success of the 5K.

On Apr 5, 2011, Lauren reaffirmed what I already knew:

"Susan is a good friend to you. Approaches you with joy in her heart."

Planning for the second annual 5K in honor of Lauren took a lot of time and energy, and it helped to be able to positively direct my emotions. But there were times when I felt so discouraged that I wanted to throw in the towel and quit However, I continued because I knew what I was doing was important to Lauren.

After that second 5K in June 2008, Susan decided the committee needed a few days of rest and relaxation. She took us to her family's beautiful home in North Carolina. Even though we arrived the day before hurricane Hannah, the trip was just what the doctor ordered. After working so hard to make the event in Lauren's honor perfect, we needed time to unwind and have fun and nothing was going to stop us, not even a hurricane. It was great to get away from home and spend time in such a serene and beautiful place with caring friends.

I visited Debbie before leaving for North Carolina because I needed to communicate with Lauren. I wanted to find out what Lauren thought about her second 5K and my upcoming trip.

"Say 'hi' to the '5K girls' and thank them for taking you on a trip. Look for me in the waves of the ocean. Watch the sunrise with me. Cool things will happen on the trip. Don't hold your friend's hand too tight on the plane. Our love is like the sun is to the ocean."

I always reviewed Lauren's messages carefully, trying to read between the lines. I knew she always was giving me clues so that I would pay closer attention. I wondered what she meant when she said, "Don't hold your friend's hand too tight on the plane," and I was somewhat bothered. Although I do hate to fly, I had managed to put the fear out of my mind by shopping and packing for the trip. I should've known Lauren's message was a clue. Sure enough, on our flight to North Carolina, the plane hit a pocket of turbulence and took a huge dip. Without thinking about it, I grabbed my friend's hand and squeezed it tightly. It wasn't until the next day that I remembered what Lauren had said about the flight.

Early in the morning on the second day of our trip, Susan found an email on her mobile device, with the subject line, "Thank you." But the sender of the message was unknown, and the email disappeared from the phone shortly after she received it. Susan told me she knew in her heart the message was from Lauren in appreciation for getting me to take a much-needed vacation.

On the last day of the trip, I was abruptly awakened at 5:30 a.m. It was as if someone shook me awake. I immediately remembered Lauren's message to watch the sunrise with her. I had forgotten and now it was our last day there. I quietly and hurriedly dressed so I wouldn't wake anyone else. I grabbed my disposable camera and headed down to the beach. There wasn't another soul there. The view was breathtaking. I sat on the steps of the dock snapping some of the most beautiful photos of the sunrise I had ever seen.

I didn't see any signs of Lauren at the time, but when I had the pictures developed, my gift was revealed. It's amazing what a disposable camera can capture when there's an angel involved. The photograph showed angel wings hugging the entire ocean. It's framed and hanging on my living room wall with an inscription of one of the sentences from Lauren's message I received before the trip:

"Our love is like the sun is to the ocean."

During a channeling session after the trip, Lauren reaffirmed her message:

"Mom, there are angels on the water."

25

Janice

Lauren brought Debbie and me closer together as friends. Debbie once remarked that she felt as if Lauren were her daughter, too. One evening, I met Debbie for dinner and I invited her to come to my home afterwards since she had never been there.

When we were seated at our table, I noticed Debbie had a gift bag. My birthday was the previous week and I assumed the gift was for me. We talked for a while before Debbie reached for the bag. She said she wanted to give me something for my birthday but couldn't decide what to buy. Instead, she channeled Lauren. I was so excited about receiving a gift from my girl on my birthday that I could hardly control my emotions. How thoughtful of Debbie, taking time out of her busy schedule to contact Lauren. I opened the bag and found a scroll secured by a beautiful gold butterfly. I unrolled it and began to read:

"My mom is doing better; she likes life better now. Some days will be hard for her, like my birthday. I comfort you,

Mom. I come to you in ways that you know it's me. I lift your spirits because I know you need it. You miss Grandma and Grandpa. They miss you, too. But they are in love and peace. They know their daughter does the best she can to hold things together. She wishes that things were better, but knows that they aren't; that they can't be changed. They wished they could have gone before me. They know it was in God's plan. This is your special day. Shine, Mom. Swirls of darkness will fade. Moments will get happier. Memories will solidify into comfort. Not the same as having me there, but moments that will comfort you. Parade through life with your head held high. You are the best, Jan Kiefer, you're my mom I love you."

What a wonderful gift. Just a "Hello, Mom, I love you. I'm fine," would've been enough to make me happy. But this message even told me Lauren was with Nani and Baba. I couldn't thank Debbie enough.

When I finished reading Lauren's message, I noticed Debbie had a small spot of light on her face. However, the lighting in the restaurant hadn't changed.

"You have a spotlight shining on your face," I told her, as I looked around the restaurant. But I couldn't determine the source of the light.

"I don't see it or feel it," Debbie said, looking in a mirror.

"Are you sure you can't see that light?" From my vantage point, it was right in the center of Debbie's face, covering her eyes, and nose.

We ate dinner, but the light was very distracting, making it hard for me to focus on our conversation. I also felt as if I was being tickled the whole evening, especially around my ankles. But still, we managed to talk for quite some time. The conversation eventually and inevitably focused on Lauren and what happened the night she was killed.

Debbie had previously asked whether I wanted to hear what happened. "As Lauren's mom," she said at the time, "you have the right to know. It's your choice."

Half of me wanted to know, but the other half knew it would be too upsetting to hear what Debbie had to say. At the same time I felt if Lauren could go through what she did that Christmas, I certainly could take some of the pain and hear what happened. I nodded my head.

Debbie began to explain what happened, then suddenly pulled back and stopped talking. "Lauren just splashed water on my face," she said, shocked and surprised. "She doesn't want us to talk about this."

"You're kidding." I said.

But no, Debbie was not kidding. Every time we attempted to continue the conversation something very strange happened to Debbie. I watched in horror as she crouched down in the booth, suddenly looking pale, seemingly ill. Her entire expression changed. I became frightened. I didn't know whether Debbie was in pain. I wondered if maybe she was having a heart attack. Debbie closed her eyes. She seemed to be in a trance. She was actually sweating.

"Deb, are you okay?" I nervously asked her. "Are you sick?"

If I hadn't witnessed the change in Debbie with my own two eyes, I would've never believed this really happened. The episode lasted for a couple of minutes. When Debbie came out of the trance, she repeated: "Lauren doesn't want us talking about this."

"No, no, we will never talk about it again," I said. "Knowing what happened will not bring Lauren back. I'm so sorry. Are you okay? Can you tell me what happened to you?"

"Tonight has been very emotional for me," Debbie replied. "I'm sorry. I don't feel well enough to go to your house."

Just then, we both jumped, feeling as if we received a light shock; like a pin sticking us in the chest. I know this sounds unbelievable but it's true. I couldn't fabricate this if I tried. How could I possibly explain something like this, except to tell what really happened? I felt so awful that Lauren had used such drastic measures to stop Debbie from telling me details about that horrific Christmas Day. This woman had helped us so unselfishly. I apologized numerous times to Debbie, because I felt responsible for Lauren's actions. My daughter was in heaven, and I was apologizing for her behavior. How crazy!

After about 20 minutes Debbie said she was finally feeling better. When we parted that evening, I was so upset leaving her, not knowing what she was really thinking about the whole situation. When I got home, I found myself reliving every horrible moment of that Christmas evening Lauren was taken. I thought for sure this would be the last time I saw Debbie. Not only was I losing my gateway to Lauren, but also a new friendship.

During the week that followed, I told Lauren what she did to Debbie was wrong. "Debbie is the person helping us to communicate," I said. "She's gone through a lot to help us, and she is our friend."

I knew in my heart that Lauren didn't mean to hurt anyone. She really didn't know her own strength. Considering where she was, how could anyone possibly be mad at her? I realized Lauren's love for me was her motivation for stopping Debbie. Lauren was just trying to protect me because she knew I would be upset after Debbie told me what happened. I know now that Lauren will protect me whenever it's within her power. She's so determined and she loves me infinitely.

JANICE

Debbie called me at the end of the week. I was ecstatic when I heard her voice. Lauren had come to her with a message:

"Please still take care of my mom."

Lauren actually listened when I told her what she did was wrong; she knew how upset I was. I'm grateful she positively responded.

26

Janice

In July 2008, I planned a trip to California for a week to visit long-time friends. I was looking forward to sitting on the beach, enjoying the sun and the ocean. Taking vacations away helped me to stop focusing on the horror of Lauren's death.

I had a channeling session with Debbie before leaving for California to see what Lauren had to say about my trip. Lauren knew how leery I was about flying, and this trip was my first time flying alone. Lauren communicated to me through Debbie:

"It's good that you're going away. Quit worrying about your trip. Hold my hand on the plane. But I won't be your stewardess."

"Will you be there with me?" I asked.

"I am everywhere. You are keeping me alive with your love."

One evening during my trip, my friends and I went out to dinner. There were six of us at the table. It was wonderful to be with old friends. We had so much to talk about and catch up on, and the conversation was quite lively. While we were talking, the chandelier in the center of the room caught my eye. I noticed that the lights were dimming very low and then shining very brightly. My mind began to wander, as it always does when lights start flickering. I began to think that maybe Lauren was trying to get my attention. As I continued to think about Lauren and how much I missed her, the lights continued alternating between dimming very low and shining brightly. I became apprehensive and wondered if Lauren was trying to warn me of something. Even though it might seem crazy, my daughter and I truly understood each other.

I was so distracted by the lights and the feeling of missing Lauren that I stopped paying attention to the conversation, which went on for a few hours. I wanted to know if Lauren was trying to reach me. Thinking about her, I asked: "Honey if you have something to say, please call Debbie."

The lights continued to flicker for another hour and I couldn't believe that no one else noticed them. When it was time to leave, I checked my cell phone to find out the time. The caller-ID showed there was a message from Debbie. My heart dropped to my feet as I ran outside to return her call. It was 9 p.m. in California, which meant it was 11 p.m. in Illinois. As I returned Debbie's call, I hoped she'd still be awake. I didn't want to miss a message from my dear daughter.

Debbie answered the telephone sounding wide awake. "I'm sorry to bother you on your vacation, but Lauren came to me with a message for you."

Debbie always apologized when she called, even though I

did my best to reassure her that she was never a bother. I always was elated to hear those words, "Lauren came to me with a message for you," and I listened intently to my daughter's message:

"My mom is so depressed. She thinks because she is far away, I'm not with her. Tell her I'm always with her."

I still don't have the words to explain what happened nor can I describe how I felt receiving a message from Lauren that night. There I was in California and Debbie was in Illinois, and Lauren again showed me that she was *everywhere*. Lauren tuned in to what I was thinking and feeling and knew that I needed to hear from her.

The message from Lauren eased the depression. She lifted my spirits by letting me know she was in tune with my feelings. It was so painful living without her physical presence. But she continued to give me inspiration to carry on.

My friends and I went for a walk after dinner, and I extended my hand to Lauren to walk with me. I had the biggest smile on my face, and felt so blissfully happy that my "shining star" had once again enveloped me from her world. The remainder of my vacation was wonderful.

My daughter is dead? Not in the sense that I've always thought of death. Her physical body is gone, but my daughter is so alive, whole, and very attentive to my needs.

⸎

Lauren continued to contact Debbie when she sensed that I was discouraged. A few months after the second 5K, Debbie had a message for me. I was feeling defeated at the time and Lauren reached out to help me get back on track.

Sept. 20, 2008:

"The hope within my mom should not dwindle. I am gone but I am not forgotten. I am in her soul, her mind, her spirit. In your heart feel at peace, it just happened. But I AM WITH YOU AND DOING WORK THROUGH YOU. I SHOW YOU LIGHT. Don't despair. We have work to do. We have sunshine to follow. We have lives to renew. You must go on, you must have hope. Pull from the depths of your strength. Clouds will come, but sunshine washes them away. Good prevails. Know I am with you, I am whole, I am at peace. I am working through you. I set horizons and we will accomplish them. You are my feet now, my legs, my voice to bring messages of hope to others. Through the foundation, you are following your heart. You are making hard decisions and you are standing up for yourself. Keep my wishes intact. Don't stray from the goal. Let wisdom prevail. This lady (meaning Debbie) speaks my words for you. She has hearing like other people don't. She projects my wishes."

Two days later, while Debbie was walking Sadie, Lauren contacted her again. Debbie told me she saw a shadow of writing on one of the houses she had passed, and sensed Lauren had something more to say. She checked in with Lauren as soon as she returned home.

Sept. 22, 2008:

"I miss my mom. I need to make this clear to you. We have work to do. See it in your heart to do the work, polish your pencil. Tell my mom I need her. I see her grasping for me.

JANICE

Tell her that it may not always seem it, but I am always there. I carry her with me, she carries me with her. We are like one – Frick & Frack and BB & Bobo – a mom and daughter who love each other. Our love will endure and give her strength for the road ahead, the up days and down. Strength for people who aggravate her, and the ones who bring her joy, and the ones who don't know what to say.

"*I will never let go of you, so don't worry. Our hearts are like one. I know it's hard, I miss you, too, but I see it all. Plug the holes in your heart and let others in. It will never be the same, it will just be different. See my memory, feel my presence, know I am in light. Know I'm in a place where you will be someday, where others will caress you, and you will have peace. Where the sun shines all the time, kindness and forgiveness exists, reflection abounds.*

"*Don't worry about the little things, Mom. Let them roll off your back. We know the bigger picture. We know the existence of the power of love, the power of us to 'talk,' to feel each other's presence. To have closeness and love, to have understanding in our souls for those who don't get it. Sow your dreams again, they are not dead. You will have lots of fun, happy years. You have hearts to heal that you don't know. The gift of giving in my name, in my spirit, in my absence—it gives me presence to those whose lives weren't as enriched as mine. Those who have tragedy and suffering, to those that feel hope is lost…a gift from no-where from a girl named Lauren.*

"*Oh, Mom, it's the best way through this. You will see*

the light someday when we can hold each other's hearts together. My truths and my words are not magic, it is just that your eyes are open and your heart is big and you know my songs. I am proud of you, Mom. You are my biggest supporter, my champion, my hero, my light, my savior, and my friend. Keep this lady close to you. She will speak my words to you of my plan, my wishes, my hopes. Smile when you see her. This is not easy for her."

❦

I recall Thanksgiving of 2008 being a time of sadness, and a reminder of who was missing from our family. I woke up very sad and depressed, not wanting to celebrate another holiday without Lauren. I went to the cemetery about 8:30 a.m. to visit her. I stayed awhile, telling Lauren how much I missed and loved her.

But the visit to the cemetery didn't help. I was very upset and missed Lauren even more. In desperation, I asked her to please contact Debbie. During the channeling sessions with Debbie, I really did feel as if I were having a telephone conversation with my daughter. Now, I needed Lauren to reach out to me again.

"It's Thanksgiving," I pleaded. "Please don't forget about your mom. Please call Debbie."

It seemed as if Lauren never wanted to disappoint me. My cell phone rang approximately 20 minutes later, and the caller-ID read "Debbie." Although I had asked Lauren to contact Debbie, I was actually surprised when Debbie called.

"Could this really be happening?" I thought as I reached for the phone. "Did Lauren actually hear me pleading with her to get in touch with Debbie?"

"Hello," I said as if I knew what was coming next. I listened as Debbie explained she'd been in the yard with Sadie because it was such a beautiful day.

"How are you doing?" Debbie asked.

"Not good," I responded. I waited for Debbie's response, hoping she had a message.

"Well, it's no wonder that Lauren came to me," Debbie said.

I told Debbie about my morning cemetery visit, and she said it was around the same time that Lauren communicated to her:

> *"My mom is sad to the depths of her soul. Tell her I'm always with her."*

I was so elated. I thanked Debbie over and over for calling. Those few words, just knowing that Lauren could hear me and that she was always near, helped to bring me out of depression. Lauren, with the help of Debbie, made my Thanksgiving bearable.

Lauren always had a way of bringing me out of the deepest darkness and into the brightest light. I thought to myself at that moment: "My daughter is a miracle." And then I said aloud to Lauren: "You are so amazing, you are my hero."

That was only the beginning of Lauren helping to assure that I would be in a better state of mind that Thanksgiving weekend.

༄

I received several catalogs every week through the mail. During one of the sessions with Debbie, Lauren communicated out of the blue:

> *"Mom you get so many catalogs."*

I reminded Lauren how she and Carli used to receive department store catalogs for Christmas from Nani every year when they were little girls. Lauren and Carli loved playing cutouts with the catalogs, especially with the brides. But at the time Lauren mentioned my receiving a lot of catalogs, I had no idea that would be a clue. As I was soon to learn, Lauren often planted seeds to make me more aware of what she was doing.

About four months before Thanksgiving, I began receiving department store catalogs addressed to me. But under my name was printed, Annt: Debbie, which I thought was an abbreviation for "Attention: Debbie." I took the first of many catalogs to show Debbie. She was even shocked, saying, "That girl will do anything to get my attention."

Even though Lauren had lifted my spirits with her message, Thanksgiving weekend still felt long. I decided to purchase something from a catalog for a "quick fix." I called to order a wall sconce I had been admiring.

"Can I have the numbers on the back of your catalog please?" the woman on the phone asked.

I read her the numbers. She recited my address. "Correct," I replied.

"Lauren?" she asked.

"No." I said. "This is Janice." I was taken aback. How cruel of her to ask me if I was Lauren. But then I realized the woman on the phone had no way of knowing about Lauren. At that moment, I also remembered the catalog I was using had Debbie's name on it.

"How did you get Lauren's name, ma'am?" I asked.

"Is she your daughter?"

"Yes."

"She must have just ordered from your catalog."

"Oh, okay," I replied.

My "rock star" had just outdone herself. The catalog was mailed to my new address; a place I moved to three months after Lauren's passing. I hung up the phone and began to laugh out loud. I was elated and amazed, to say the least.

"How do you do these things?" I asked Lauren. "You'd better be careful or you could be arrested for mail fraud." I jokingly said aloud.

Lauren's message on Thanksgiving and the catalog incident the next day took me from tears to laughter. To this day, I still receive catalogs with the notation, "Annt: Debbie." I have a collection of them from three different department stores. They are all gifts from Lauren. Whenever I receive them, I feel blessed and laugh out loud. I'm sure that's what she had in mind.

Lauren's antics with the mail didn't stop with this incident. A few weeks later, Jeanne called me to say she received the "ab work out" tapes she had ordered from an infomercial.

"Something is weird," she said to me about the order. "The package was addressed to Uncle Louie." Our Uncle Louie was living in a nursing home at the time.

"Did you use Uncle Louie's credit card?" I asked.

"No," she replied. "He doesn't have a credit card. The invoice has my name, address and credit card number on it. But it's to the attention of Uncle Louie."

"How could that happen?"

We were both silent for a moment, then began laughing. Our darling girl was at it again.

⚜

The week before Christmas, Debbie channeled Lauren. Her message was:

"Wear my necklace, Mom. I was preparing you. Don't

hate Christmas, Mom. God doesn't want you to."

"Well, He shouldn't have taken you away from me," I responded.

"That was decided a long time ago. I miss you, but you make it bearable by going to Debbie and talking to me. We walk in the sunshine together. We will be together some day again. But don't make it too soon. I can only be with you in a certain way, and don't be in a hurry to be with me in the same way."

"I want to be with you but I don't want to leave here yet."

"It's a journey that we all take. I was prepared; I wasn't scared. I had God's hand. I felt your love all the way. All the love that you've shown me since I was little. Your love raised me up to help me make the transition. You are my strength. My spirit would not be complete without knowing that you love me.

"No one could love you more than me."

"You and God provided me with a beam of light. The source of all goodness. My hand was not empty. You're the one who had the hard journey, dealing with the police.

"The only hard journey I had was losing you."

"I rose quickly, painlessly. Solace is mine."

27

Janice

Lauren continued to send "gifts" throughout the holiday season. When I saw her father on Christmas he mentioned he had been receiving a trade magazine addressed to Lauren Kiefer.

"That stunt has 'Trixy' written all over it," I said.

"What do you mean?" he asked. "I've just been tossing them."

I told Nick about all the catalogs. "Keep the magazines," I said. "They're a gift from Lauren."

Nick scanned the cover of the magazine and sent it to me. Just as he said, it was addressed to Lauren Kiefer at his address. Lauren "distributed" these gifts within five weeks of each other – all during the holiday season. I know she was making sure we all got to share her beautiful essence, and I'm sure Lauren wanted to show she could still make us laugh during our hardest of times.

During a later channeling session with Debbie, I asked Lauren if she was responsible for the way our mail was addressed.

"Yes," she replied. "I'm good aren't I? I rock!"

"How did you do that?" I asked.

"I can't tell you. You run around like nuts. I have to get your attention some way. I steal things, I play jokes, I maneuver things, I bring you joy, I bring you light, I bring you honor and all the people that show you how much they love me."

๛

After Christmas, Carli and I headed to Florida to stay with our cousin and Lauren's Godfather, Steve, and his wife, Erin. Even though my goal was to get away from it all, I could never leave behind thoughts of Lauren. Our lives had been turned upside down without her. The thoughts and feelings followed me wherever I went.

I was also still thinking about the most recent communication I had with Lauren:

"Have a good time in Florida."

"Will you go with us?" I asked her.

"Nothing can stop me. Watch the sunset with me in Florida. Our toes will touch in the sand. Bring some sunscreen and a hat so your color doesn't fade."

"You are my keeper, Laurie. You take such good care of me."

"It's not always easy. Parents usually guide kids, but now I'm guiding you. I'm pretty good at it. People here your age tell me I'm a good daughter. They feel about their kids

there the way you feel about me here."

Lauren's personality was ever-present during those channeling sessions. Although Lauren's vocabulary changed in many ways after transcending, her essence was still evident. She was aware of everything and she had become an authority on all subjects. She was very opinionated, but her wisdom was also astounding. My darling little daughter, who at times I used to think of as a "scatterbrain," was now my keeper and my teacher. I felt so blessed to have my own personal guardian angel.

When we arrived in Florida, we headed to the beach. I immediately felt Lauren's presence with us. Before we could even set our chairs down, we saw a darling little girl running all over the beach. Her mother was chasing after her, calling out her name. I thought I heard the girl's name correctly, but I asked the mom to be sure.

"What's your daughter's name?" I asked.

"Lauren" she replied.

We all glanced at each other, knowing that Lauren was with us. The little girl's antics actually reminded me of my little Lauren; how she would act up and run away from me. Watching that little girl made me think about something Lauren said during the channeling session before Christmas:

"Remember mom when you used to yell at me on the beach, 'Don't drown! Don't drown!'"?

"Yes, I remember that, Laur," I said. "You always went out way too far in the ocean."

"I was a tease and a taunt, I was bratty. I had a special way of knowing what was inside of people. I was wild. I

was a tomboy, cuts, scrapes, bruises, knocks. I was nuts. Who cared? I had fun. I was full of energy."

Lauren also mentioned a woman in Florida whose name began with "L." During the session, Debbie asked if I knew such a person.

"Maybe Lauren is referring to one of Steve and Erin's friends," I told Debbie at the time. "I don't know anyone in Florida."

Based on Lauren's message, I was anxious to watch the sunset with her. I knew there would surely be a message from her in the sunset photos I was planning to take.

Finally, the last day of our vacation, we arranged to watch the sunset with Steve and Erin's friends, whom we met on the way to the beach. One of the women was named Lynette, which solved the mystery of Lauren's message about the woman whose name began with the letter "L." We all sat on the beach together talking, taking photos and watching the sun slowly descend into the ocean.

"I've watched the sunset every evening since I've been here," Lynette mentioned to us. "However, today is the first time there've been clouds in the sky."

At that moment, I started putting Lauren's clues together. Of course, you can't have angels in the sky without clouds— their wings would not have been visible.

When we returned home after our five-day trip, Erin emailed the sunset photos she took on our last night there. One of the photos really stood out. If we hadn't been talking so much, we probably would have caught the other wing before it dipped under water.

During the first channeling session with Debbie after my trip, Lauren said:

"Did you get my sign in the photos? I was touching Carli in the sunshine."

When I got my pictures processed, I discovered that a ray of sunshine had come right up on the beach and touched Carli. I didn't see that ray on the beach when I was taking the photograph. I have since added this picture to the collection of photos of the wondrous gifts Lauren has so generously given me.

INFINITY

28
Janice

In a message in the Spring 2009, Lauren communicated to me:

"I walk with you everywhere. I touch your hands, your heart, and your ears. I don't want to tickle you too much. Is it too much...is it okay?"

"Yes, it's okay," I said. "You can touch me anytime you want to."

"Call on me when you need me. I have peace to offer you. Far away, but nearby. Someone to behold as a light in your soul. Walk with your arms outstretched, don't close up. Life dealt you a bad deal, but you're strong and you know I am in your life. I'm here to honor your presence. To awaken the spirit in you to help do my work. You must live each day in happiness. I stockpiled and I had this great reservoir of love when I was there and that's why it's over-flowing now, because the reservoir was so full. So don't be sad about my passing. It was meant to be."

"It's so hard, Laur."

"You need to reflect me (her goodness). I was a spark of energy to be reckoned with."

"You are a beautiful spark. You're a sweetheart."

"You had me, Mom. You have the strength, too. You join me in peace. A mother and daughter so close, no one can separate them. An unstoppable duo."

❧

When days have passed and I haven't felt Lauren's presence, I ask: "Where are you Laur? I can't feel you here. I need to know that you're near."

I received my answer when Debbie facilitated a session between us a few months later:

"I wish I could see you," I told Lauren.

"Mom, I'm in your eyes. I do what I can. I'm a messenger with skills not like everyone has. I'm a deliverer of peace to you. There may be silent times that I don't come to you, but don't worry. I'll come back. I am blessed with you, so I will bless you with me."

"You are my blessing, Laurie."

"I work miracles through you. I tell them here about how loving you are. I tell them how I cross over."

"How do you do that?

"God helps me and this lady, too. I didn't know this lady when I was there."

Debbie and I laugh when Lauren refers to her as "this lady," but I remind Debbie it's also a sign of affection.

"I love you, Mom, and I love Debbie, too. Debbie is my friend. She is a beautiful gift. Your fate was met when you were 16, for you to come back together now, to help one another. She lost her daughter, too. Debbie's and your heart touched in high school; a journey to be had later. Two souls reunited by tragedy. I use Debbie to get my words known. She's an angel to me."

$\sim$

In a subsequent channeling session Lauren said out of the blue:

"I called you the other night."

One day headed to work, I forgot to bring along my cell phone. I found it on my nightstand when I returned home later that day. I discovered Debbie had called.

"Did you call me or did Lauren?" her message said. I laughed as I called Debbie back, and explained to her that I had forgotten my cell phone that morning.

"The call came from your cell phone," Debbie said. "My screen lit up with 'Janice,' and then your name quickly disappeared."

"We are blessed with a gift that not everyone gets, and you get it from our love and being open to it. We are so lucky. It

won't stop, it's in our hearts. It's different, but I am always with you. Pure love brings it."

❧

Sept. 28, 2009:

"I have fun in heaven. Suffering on earth. Earth is just a place where we do our job to get to heaven. It's just a minute in an eternity. I have palaces in the sky. It's so beautiful. There is no time source here."

"Are you happy, Laur?" I asked.

"Not the same happy as you know. It's glorious; calm, serene, retrospective, ethereal, heaven-like. When I look back at my life, it is like a scene from a movie. I almost knew I wouldn't be on earth long, so I had to pack a lot into my time."

"I almost knew too, but I didn't want to know."

At that moment, Debbie saw Lauren skipping through a beautiful field of flowers, with her blonde hair flowing, and making snow angels in the field. This was so heart-wrenching. But I felt Lauren was happy and at peace. I tried to forget about my own earthly wishes and desires of needing her here with me.

❧

What I'm learning and understanding from the channeling sessions is that when you pass from earth your job is not finished. In several of Lauren's messages, she talked about her job in Heaven and I could see that she's still very busy.

June 30, 2008:

"There are avenues in Heaven and people still have to make choices. God loves us all. You have to find your way in heaven. Nani is with the older people and I am with the younger people, but we all work in a circle."

Nov. 8, 2008:

"I am taking care of babies here. That is my job. I see the light in their eyes; the innocence in their voices, their grasp of pure joy. Some are crawling. Mom, now I know how much patience you had to have when I was little. I walked a long way today, the kids keep me going."

"I'm so happy that you are a mom," I said.

"If I was a mom there, I would be getting my nails done all the time."

Lauren and I actually joked about this very thing before she passed. We talked about her having children someday, and how she would probably be the type of mother who was always getting her nails done.

"Lauren, I love you," I said.

"Oh, Mom, you know I love you, too, forever and ever. Walk with me, talk with me, sing with me. Know I am with you, smile our smile. When you smile, I smile through

you. I top off your day with kisses to you.

"My world is different here, but I'm trying to make yours better there."

I often had wondered what was going on where Lauren was; I imagined there had to be a whole other life there. After Lauren's explanation, I felt as if I'd had a glimpse of Heaven.

❧

During a channeling session in August 2008, Lauren talked about her grandpa and grandma after they passed.

Aug. 28, 2008:

"Whisper your wishes to me. Nani hears them too. They talk about you and say how lucky they were to have you, a loving girl.

"Nani and Baba are more reserved here. I am more active."

Nani had something during a later channeling session in May:

"Your father and I were blessed with two beautiful girls. We are happy and in solace."

"Are you taking care of Laurie, Mom?" I asked her.

"Laurie is taking care of us."

"How is she, Mom?"

JANICE

"She is the same, beautiful and sparkly as ever. She's a gem among us. One who can go back (come back to me). She works with kids, young ones that have passed."

I truly felt blessed that evening by the visit with my daughter, my mom and my dad, all together, the way it used to be. I couldn't recall the last time I had such a peaceful feeling.

∽∾

My friend Joni, who delivered the cherub lawn ornament on Lauren's behalf, visited her family in Hawaii in 2009. When she returned home from her trip, she came to see me.

"Janny, I saved this story to tell you in person, Joni said.

I was so excited and anxiously asked, "Lauren?"

"I think so."

Joni and I sat at my kitchen table and she told me what happened in Hawaii: "I was sitting on my lanai on the seventh floor, looking at the ocean and thinking of Lauren. Along came a white dove. It stopped in midair, flapping its wings close to my face and stared at me. Then it perched itself on the railing. It turned its head from side to side, and continued looking at me." Joni showed me the dove's motions with her hands. The bird stayed for at least 10 minutes, she said.

"Were you frightened?" I asked.

"Yes, at first. Then I said, 'Lauren?' The dove didn't move. I ran to get my digital camera. When I returned it was still there perched on the railing. I actually felt peaceful when I realized that it was Lauren. I even took five pictures of the dove so that I could bring the photos home to show you."

Joni sounded very excited as she took out her digital camera. But when she flipped through the files on her camera, she couldn't find the photos of the dove. All of the other pictures from her vacation were there except the bird.

"Laur, what did you do with those pictures?" Joni said laughing. She turned to me. "Don't worry. I've already downloaded them to my computer. I'll email the photos to you in the morning."

While Joni was telling me this story, the most amazing thing happened. The light in the kitchen ceiling dimmed very low and then illuminated brightly. I knew Lauren was telling us, "Make no mistake, it's me!"

How remarkable. Joni and I cried. It was such a beautiful moment knowing Lauren was actually with us, and confirming what she had done.

It was no surprise to me when Joni emailed me the next day to say the photos of the dove were gone from her computer, too. However, Lauren did not erase the photo of the dove Joni took with her cell phone, so I finally got to see it. We laughed so hard at how amazing my daughter is. I asked Joni to send the dove's photo to my phone in hopes of including a copy of it in this book. But no matter how hard Joni tried, even enlisting help at a photo finishing store, she could not send it to me or print a copy of the photograph of the dove.

I was finally able to ask Lauren about the bird during a channeling session:

May 7, 2009:

"Laurie, did you make the bird fly away on Joni?"

"The white one?"

"Yes, the white one."

JANICE

"I wanted to give Joni hope"

"You did, Laurie, and you gave me hope, too."

"Aren't I creative? I'm a trickster."

Lauren knew Joni was a genuine and fun-loving person and would get her message to me.

29

Janice

On Lauren's birthday, Feb. 25, 2009, I visited Debbie so I could once again feel near to Lauren and celebrate her birthday with her. I noticed a change in Lauren's communication between 2008 and 2009. It seemed to me that she had become more accustomed to where she was.

I was very impatient, lying on the table waiting for her spirit to arrive. I was thinking to myself, "Laur, please come, I need to speak to you." I was always so anxious during the channeling sessions waiting for her to communicate, and hoping that the bridge between her world and mine had not closed.

It took a little longer during this session for Lauren to respond and when she did, she sounded a little impatient with me. Her words felt so familiar and it felt exactly as if she was here.

"Geez, Mom, slow down, slow down, I'll be there."

"I miss you. Happy birthday, Honey."

When I said "happy birthday" this time, Lauren did not ask us to sing to her.

"I have all happy days now. No pain, no sorrow, no worry. Wishes for you though not to worry. Don't be sad about my birthday. I'm ageless now."

In each of the channeling sessions, my main concern was for Lauren's well-being and happiness. Was she yearning for us the way we were yearning for her? Was she angry because of what happened? Was she afraid? Did she long to be with her family and friends? Was she mourning us the way that we were mourning her?

Those questions haunted me daily. Lauren was so young and vibrant when she left us, and now that she was communicating with me, I thought for sure, she also had all of those same feelings. It disgusted me to think of what she was missing. She was taken away so young, in the prime of her life, with so much to look forward to. I needed the answers to those questions, if I was ever to have some sort of peace in my life.

I was elated to hear from Lauren during that session that she was always happy. She helped me immensely by letting me know she had transcended beyond the physical and emotional pain of what she went through that Christmas night.

At the same time, however, I had an empty feeling. I felt as if she didn't need me at all anymore and her birthdays were happy without us, her family. I realized during this session that I needed Lauren more than she needed me. It had become a complete role reversal.

"There is no pain, no longing, just beauty, comfort and light, love, gold, angels, no hurts, no pain, no battles,

peace. My heart is full of butterflies. The angels help me. I am still bringing joy where I am. Look at all we had, Mom.

"I know it's hard for you there, I peek at you through shadows. You are my life, my savior, my rock, my blessing; my one who stayed with me no matter what. You help make what I want to happen, happen. We are a team, like 'Frick and Frack' and 'BB and BoBo.'"

"I couldn't do it without you," I told Lauren.

"It's all rolled into love and knowing we're on the right path. We have special moments of loneliness, and I hope the little things I do help you."

"They help me so much, Laurie, thank you. I just want one more day with you."

"We'll be together, Mom. But don't hurry.

30

Janice

Lauren's message on Dec. 15, 2009, one week before the third anniversary of her passing, helped to comfort me during the holiday season. I have never felt as close to Lauren as I do now.

"It's dark for you there, but light for me here. It's a journey. I bless you every day. I wish happiness for you. Through petals of flowers I blow kisses to you. I am running my fingers through your hair and I feel you running your fingers through my hair. It's been a while since I've been gone from there, but it doesn't seem that long to me.

"I am balanced now. I have one foot here and one foot there. I'm accomplishing it. I bridge between here and there. I cancel all your sorrow. Our rivers flow together. Our energies are meeting. You're the catalyst of my book. I am a light for you. You have a slice of heaven in your heart. You are my protector, you are a gracious gift. My heart lies open in your hands. You're sunshine in my heart. A whisper in your ear, a tickle in your hair, a spot of light

*on the wall. A brush against your face, an indentation on
your pillow. I do it to keep your heart going!*

*"It's not the same, but I'm there. A whisk in the wind, a
ripple in the ocean, a spot on the grass, a cover on a book.
A spark to light other's eyes. Of wisdom, of courage, of how
well you loved, as a tribute to me. As a beacon for others to
guide them through horror. A light to soothe their soul. A
picture of a girl who was wild, but turned out pretty darn
good. A little brat that ran you around like a knucklehead.
I drove you crazy."*

Lauren's words were poetic, insightful and comforting; a
blessing beyond description.

Other times during the channeling session, the teasing
manner Lauren used to communicate with me showed her true
personality. Playfulness was a part of her true essence, and hearing about it during the session was as familiar to me as it was
when she was here.

*"When I was little I had bubblegum in my hair. I wasn't
afraid of anything, I was a tomboy. I had curly hair when
I was little."*

The descriptions Lauren shared were all true; she always
described herself perfectly as she was here on earth. She also
talked about her teen and young adult years:

*"I was the hot chick in heels. I could get what I wanted by
smiling, not mean. I always wanted thinner legs."*

When Lauren complained about her legs, I always reassured her that her legs were just fine

"What was I thinking when I smoked?

"I used to pretend to cook when I was little, then I played for real in a restaurant. I worked hard at the bar, but it was fun. Nice customers. The Fitz's were good to me."

Sometimes, Lauren even talked about her pink lipstick, which she liked instead of orange:

"I liked to match my lips to my nails."

"I still have your nail polish, Laur," I shared with her.

"Get rid of it. We don't need nail polish here. We have something you can't see or feel but it's in our hearts."

Often, the messages Lauren shared were full of profound insights about herself and about her life:

"You and Dad had to be patient with me. I was a hand-ful, but I turned out great. I was a spark of energy to be reckoned with. I had beauty, but the modeling was not my calling. It was a way of getting people's attention. A gateway to their souls. My looks would make them listen. I could see through people, but I didn't say it so much. Others liked me, I saw their heart. I wanted to get to know them inside. I could sense their sadness and desperation and I prayed for them.

"I made my friends laugh. I was a clown, but I refused to

wear clown shoes. I was a spitfire in good shoes. Leopard, stylish. Checks would go right for clothes. I called you sometime and asked if I could charge something. I'd be in fancy shoes, but sometimes I felt like I had two left feet. I'm smart. I didn't want anyone manipulating me in the modeling though. I had to wear some outfits I didn't like. I'm my own person."

I still had many fond memories of the times Lauren and I spent together when she worked as a model.

"We had fun with modeling, didn't we?" I reminded her.

"Glamour. Have your conscience be at ease. You did every-thing right with me, and I was trying. I was a little brat, and I drove you nuts. Sleepless nights, waiting up for me, afraid to go to bed until I got home from work."

"I always worried about you. You were so special."

"God knew it. Peaceful times were not always had at the Kiefer house. I like how you portray me in your story. Fun, but also helping others. And yes, I was drawn to the church by God. I had a calling. I spoke words to so many. Touched so many. Now I do work behind the scenes, still helping friends and family.

"I remember feeling warm when I was inside you. I was created to get to know people and what was inside of them. I called you my best friend.

"Some people thought I was an air head, a pretty face with

*nothing up there. I was devoted to family. I was sarcastic
sometimes. I loved life. Keep your spirits high. Your smiles
will remind you of me."*

Lauren would get paid on Friday, and head right to her
favorite clothing and shoe store.

*"I had a shoe fetish, a shopaholic lady who liked her
clothes, some credit card issues, and lots of saying. 'Oh,
Mom, it will be okay.'*

*"I gave you your shoe fetish. Did Car buy those hot shoes
at Carson's?"*

It just so happened, Carli and I had been shopping at
Carson's the night before the channeling session. Whenever
Carli and I spend time together, I always ask Lauren to be with
us, and I just knew she was always there. I *did* buy Carli a pair
of shoes for her birthday that evening. In fact, Carli and I have
never cared about shoes as much as we do now. We can't walk
into a store without heading to the shoe department, to purchase shoes we must have, but surely don't need. I now have a
closet full of shoes that I don't even wear.

❧❧

Another funny incident that Lauren repeatedly referred to
during the channeling sessions involved her Godfather, Steve.
I was sitting on the couch in the living room of my new place,
talking to Steve and his wife, Erin. Steve was hanging curtain
rods, while Erin and I talked about furnishings. We were discussing how I should've purchased a variety of colors for the
couch's accent pillows, instead of all navy blue. We were going

back and forth about which colors would have been better. The more we talked, the more I realized the mistake I made buying only navy blue pillows.

I didn't have to worry about my mistake for long, because my little trickster remedied the situation. When I woke up the next day and walked downstairs to the living room, I immediately noticed that one of the navy blue pillows was missing. I originally had six pillows on the couch, but now there were only five. It was very strange. I searched and searched. I moved the couch thinking the pillow might've fallen behind it while Steve was installing the valance rods. I got a flashlight and searched under the couch. I checked in the garbage; every closet, and the garage. Finally, I called Steve and asked whether he'd inadvertently taken the blue pillow.

"No, Jan," Steve said sarcastically. "It doesn't match my furniture."

I thought I was losing my mind as I searched every inch of my house during the next two months. I never took any of my furnishings outside, so I couldn't imagine how it disappeared. Then it dawned on me: Lauren. I kept tossing it over and over in my mind, not really believing that Laur could possibly get a pillow out of the house. However, she confirmed my suspicions during a later channeling session:

"Did you take my blue pillow?" I asked her.

"Yes. A trickster, I take pillows. Blue. Hidden as a trick."

"How do you do those things, Laur?"

"I can't tell you."

Debbie and I of course laughed and were amazed once again by Lauren's abilities. And I'm sure Lauren had a good laugh as she watched me for months searching the same areas of the house for that pillow.

The disappearance of the pillow was even more remarkable when I realized Lauren possibly took my leftover steak from Carli's kitchen counter. I had left it wrapped on the counter next to my purse. After dinner, Carli and I went upstairs to look at her new shoes. We were upstairs no longer than three minutes. When we returned to the kitchen, the steak was gone. We searched Carli's house for the steak, but it never turned up. This incident was both funny and very familiar. Lauren's pranks always had everyone running around in circles when she was here. The steak disappeared on the day of Baba's funeral, and I'm sure she just wanted to make us laugh.

During the channeling session, when I asked Lauren if she took the steak, she said:

"The steak is with the pillow."

Beautifully unbelievable. My shining star brought humor back into my life. Whenever I think of her antics, I smile and know, despite the transition, her personality has not changed. The steak was never found, and neither was the pillow. And it was no surprise because steak was Lauren's favorite food. My daughter is clever and her essence is magnificent.

⤜∽◦∾⤛

The fundraisers we held in Lauren's honor were always beautiful and well-attended. Invariably, I would leave the events with the awful feeling that we were only there because she wasn't. Lauren, of course, sensed my pain and reassured me that it was fine with her.

> *"Look at the party revelers. I can see it, Mom, and it's all
> good. It's because of you and my legacy. My continuing
> smiles I gave them when I was here. My heart touched
> theirs because I had no agenda. They knew I was genuine.
> I carried no grudges, no meanness. Just smiles and caring.
> I spoke truths. I saw God in other people. I carried His
> wishes in my heart and brought it out in other people. I
> made them feel good about who they were. I saw their spir-
> it. I saw their light. At the time I thought it was natural.
> But now I understand why I did it. I never hurt anyone,
> or didn't mean to. I wasn't perfect."*

31

Janice

I think it's pretty safe to say that those of us blessed with daughters soon come to the realization that these darling little creatures become our mothers at some point. It usually starts in their late teens and continues on for the rest of our days. They think we learned nothing over the years and only they have all the answers. I happen to have two of those so-called moms – Carli, here on earth giving me suggestions and expressing her opinion, and Lauren still giving me orders from where she is.

Since she passed away, Lauren has given me advice, commented on my actions, and provided me with comfort, just like a mom would do for her daughter. Her advice is always accurate, and I do my best to follow her suggestions. But I often remind her that I'm only human.

During several of the channeling sessions in which Lauren showed her concern for me, I felt as if we still lived together. Debbie and I laughed at some of Lauren's comments, even though we learned something from every comment she made:

"I walk a parallel path to you."

"You are a wonderful daughter" I said.

"It's a determined existence to be by your side. Sometimes you're a handful."

"Someone else I know was a handful, too."

"I wasn't as stubborn as you are. I am perfection. I'm a star in your sky. Now I don't measure things in time, I measure things in love. Like a river of peace where I'm at. I come back to teach you, Mom, because you taught me. Did you ever think I'd become this wise? Infinite."

"Are you happy? Are you okay?"

"Forever in peace, enlightenment. Pure joy, no fear, no prejudice, no lacking, no heartache. Just me in God's hands in a sacred light. A beckoning that called me. I am a teacher, I am a light. I am a gauge for all to learn from. I have you as my voice. You were chosen, you and me in this game of eternity. Our perfect love created what is hap-pening now. We fought, we cried, we loved. The stories of fun and silliness we all had."

"What is it with your bangs?"

Out of the blue, Lauren asked the very same question I had just asked myself while combing my hair in the mirror. I said aloud, "Laur, what is with my bangs?" I thought she might be listening and she definitely was.

"Do you like them, Laurie?"

"Oh, Mom, I like whatever you do."

In the same session, I asked Lauren if she could see what was on my roof. It was driving me crazy.

"A squirrel. Oh, Mom, don't sweat it. It's just an animal. You're overreacting! Go shopping and buy some new clothes. A lot of your clothes are worn."

Through Debbie, Lauren described a particular sweater *"with this kind of collar,"* which Debbie demonstrated with her hands.

"Get rid of it Mom, dress hip."

"Did you trip on concrete?"

"Yes, I did, and I know that you tried to help me up," I replied.

"Mishap? Mom, you are a klutz!"

"You were a klutz, too, sweetie."

"I didn't care. I had other stuff on my mind. Maybe I was klutzy, but I was beautiful. I had a magic heart. A soul that could touch others and is still touching. That could win them over even if they were crabby. I had a way with little kids."

"You still do have a magic heart, Honey."

"I'm glad you have a job….I like your new place. It is as cute as you. My friends painted it to make it more like home for you."

Lauren's friends are so loyal and attentive to my needs and did paint my new place for me.

"You need to cultivate good friendships, and put the others on the back burner. I will always be your best friend. I'll walk with you hand-in-hand; support you when you're down; make you laugh when you need to, and make you smile in silly ways. Steal some things, like pillows. Don't be afraid of the dark, Mom. You're not a wuss, you're tough! Powerful spirits are with you always, Mom, so don't be afraid. I send others to you for your protection. Don't be a scatterbrain like me. Parents guide kids, but now I'm guiding you."

"Thank you for taking such good care of me, Laurie."

"It's not always easy. God and I are taking care of you. I see the way things should be, away from the frailties of being human. Mom, you always worried about me driving, but you are such a bad driver. You drive like a bubblehead! I can't believe what you do with your cheeseburger. I see you taking the bun and ketchup off. Mom, don't eat like that if you're with a guy."

It's so true – I do take the bun and ketchup off of my cheeseburger when I'm at lunch or eating alone in my car.

"Shop more. I am always with you. Aren't you sick of me

yet? Don't pull your pants up so high. Don't grieve me. It's a terrible thing that happened, but there is nothing you could have done about it. So don't keep going over it in your head."

Lauren was always so health conscious and always physically fit. Now, she was prodding me to do the same.

"Are you getting enough cardio? Watch your fats. Why are you so afraid to go to the doctor? Stay healthy. You have work to do. Check your blood lipids. Cholesterol. Eat less fat and take care of your heart."

It was ironic receiving advice from my daughter instead of giving her advice. Just as Lauren always told me as we got ready for work and shared the same mirror, she was still telling me what to do:

"Put your hair behind your ears."

Another time, I asked Lauren if she enjoyed the concert Jeanne and I attended, because we both felt her in our hair simultaneously:

"Songs in the wind. I was the sparkle in your eyes. Do you two think you could ever go out alone? I believe in you, I walk among your sorrow and your joy with you. Your image will always be with me. We are beyond mother and daughter, we are best buds too. I feel your pulse. I wish happiness for you. Cry when you need to, but then stop. Make it short. Brush your fate with glitter, and I don't mean eye shadow, Mom."

I continuously told Lauren how much I missed and loved her during that session.

"Oh, Mom, stop!"

Those three words echoed Lauren's true personality, and as I drove home that evening. I felt elated and as if I actually visited my daughter.

❧

It's so wonderful to still have my daughter in my life. We still spend quality time together.

"I'm proud to be your daughter, annoying though that I was."

"You were not annoying. I wish you were here with me now," I said.

"Late nights, come on, Mom. Sleepovers with no sleep."

"I was an overprotective Mom."

"I'll say. Like when I would go out. List of instructions: 'Now, Laur….Do you have your license…do you have your keys?' You drove me up a wall."

Lauren reminded me she was still watching out for Carli:

"Buy Carli gifts, she needs things. Give her my share. She was my heart, my love, my life."
Of course, I don't know how long this wonderful gift "of

mothering" will last. I know that it could be taken away at any time. But until then, I will enjoy the beauty of still having communication with my girl.

$\sim\!\!\infty\!\!\sim$

During a session during the late Spring of 2009, Lauren told Debbie:

> *"I see billowing smoke. Don't freak my mom out, but tell her she needs to get a kitchen fire extinguisher. I see fire in the stove."*

That prediction bothered me because I could be pretty careless when I cook. I became very cautious after Lauren's warning, making sure I turned the burners off and did not leave the stove unattended. The weekend after the session, I was standing at the stove cooking dinner. I actually felt Lauren's entire body standing next to me, trying to push me away from the stove. My first reaction was to say, "Moos ovey," as Lauren had said to me when she was three. I moved away from the stove and thought about how remarkable it was that Lauren was trying to protect me. At that moment I realized her love and caring was infinite. I felt so blessed knowing that Lauren would protect me whenever it was in her power.

I later realized what she meant when she said she saw billowing smoke from my stove. I had been cooking an egg one morning before leaving for work, while running all over the house trying to get myself together. Suddenly I noticed that the smoke was billowing from the pan. Lauren made me stop and pay attention to what I was doing. Since that day, I cook very carefully.

There was one exception: One evening I had some friends

over and I was baking a pizza in the oven. I opened the oven door and attempted to remove the pizza with a dishtowel. What a disaster. I barely got the pizza out of the oven when half the cheese slipped off and fell on the kitchen floor. I didn't get away with it, because my sweet daughter reminded me what happened when she contacted Debbie in March 2010 with the message:

"Oven mitts, stove. Be careful when you're cooking and not grabbing things without oven mitts. You're just clumsy, Mom."

Debbie didn't understand what she meant, but I immediately recalled the cheese splattered across my kitchen floor.

Lauren gives me really good advice, and I don't get away with too much. She protects me and shows me that our love is even stronger now. Her analogies are so true and beautiful.

"Choose your friends and your shoes wisely. It's like patent leather shoes, because your friends reflect who you are. I call you sometimes, but you don't hear my voice. I pretend that you can see me. You smell the scents of flowers when I'm around. That's like my calling card to let you know I'm there. I am a source for you. To whisper back to me if you want to. To call on me to hear. 'Mom, I love you. It's suspension in time where we are now. But not to worry— we'll be together. Enjoy this time, you have work to do. What's with the frosting in your red hair? Smile when you think of me. Your tears are okay, but then shut them off. I know when you are crying.

"My heart is broken, Laur," I told her.

"I'm in there fixing it up with glue."

I asked Lauren during the June 29, 2010, channeling session if she had seen my kitchen ceiling cave in from water damage.

"Disaster! I'm hoping it didn't wreck any of my pictures."

"No, your pictures are fine."

"Beauty preserved."

During this session, Lauren was very humorous and it was such an uplifting experience for both Debbie and me.

"You are conceited, Laur," I jokingly said.

"Paleontologists will ask when they find my pictures, 'What species is she? She is beautiful!'"

"You are so funny, sweetie.

"You needed it, Mom. You worked your butt off for the race. I love to make you laugh."

∽∾

When the girls were growing up and living at home we, of course, had our differences as mother and daughters always do. I found that trying to get my point across by fighting with them really didn't work. When all else failed, I sat down and wrote them a letter, telling them my feelings and why I felt the way I did. I put the letter on their pillow in hopes they'd read it and understand my reasoning. It worked. They actually read the letters and often wrote back to share their feelings. The letters helped us to better understand each other and discuss the problem.

The letters did not stop after Lauren passed. When I realized she was able to communicate with me, I continued writing to her every day, expressing my feelings. Even if it was a short note, just to tell her I love her, she would be able to see me writing to her. She confirmed my belief during a channeling session with Debbie:

"I see you writing to me. You know how to make me happy."

On a really cold winter's night in January 2009, after working 12 hours that day, I was on my way to meet some of my co-workers at a nearby restaurant for a bite to eat. I pulled into the restaurant parking lot and parked under a light waiting for my friends to arrive, feeling so tired and blue. Of course, I was missing my girl. Then my cell phone rang. The incoming call was from Debbie. Her voice was music to my ears at that moment. She told me Lauren had contacted her with a beautiful message for me. Debbie sounded excited and asked if I had a minute to listen because she had already transcribed Lauren's beautiful words.

"Of course I have time, Deb," I replied. Then, Debbie shared Lauren's message:

Jan. 31, 2009:

"Weather the storms, Mom. You're doing good. I'm proud of you and your capacity to engage people, to hear their songs, and not let yours die. Still being empathetic, even

though your heart hurts. Being able to get through day-by-day without your little girl. Without my sunshine. But you know I am touching you. I am in your presence wherever you are. I work miracles. I know how to be with you. I know how to touch your nose and tickle your feet, and whisk your hair. You go with me. That's why you laugh, why we have our little messages, little funny to-dos, to let you know I'm around. Always in your heart and spirit and mind. I'll never leave your side. I summon soulful messages to you through this lady. From my heart to yours. Messages of no coincidence. A wish for you to know I'm there. I am always tickling your cute red hair, whispering things to you. Do you hear them? Do you know I'm saying 'I love you?' I am—from my heart to yours. Count on me, Mom, I'm always there. Love you. That's all. To my mom."

How does Lauren know when I need her the most? Her messages lift my spirits more than anything I have ever experienced. You can imagine my delight after hearing this message. The sun began shining so brightly for me on that cold winter's night. The message was so comforting to me that I continuously read it over and over.

32

Janice

Since receiving the first message from Lauren through Debbie in 2007, I've continued to ask myself, "Why me" and "What does this mean?" As always, I'm sure Lauren anticipated these questions, and she used the channeling sessions to both explain and share her vision:

> *"I picked you a long time ago to be my mom. I filled your soul with fun and laughter. My life was a minute there. This was my destiny. God sometimes does that. My life was taken as somewhat of a sacrifice because I do more good from where I am at. I made such an impact."*

How could I question this? God wanted Lauren on Christmas 2006. No matter how I sorted through the events over and over in my mind, I knew in my heart that God wanted Lauren. He had bigger plans for her.

Of course, I will never get over losing her. I miss her every minute of every day. But I now realize that I could not have changed her fate in any way.

"A seed of love was planted on earth with me, and it is still growing. You are my life's course. We're hand in hand in this venture. A little light and a big light. I see things you don't. I see bitterness in people and feel so sorry for them. I saw it when I was there and wanted to fix everyone. You're fixing them now."

Who receives a gift like this? I constantly ask myself this question. Surely not everyone who has lost their child has a relationship with them like I have with Lauren. I turned to my daughter to help me unravel the mystery.

"We don't all know the answers. I know I can touch people from here because of you, Mom. Because of your love and kindness and gratitude for all of those around you. Your wishes in the night that I could come back. You know I can't. But you know that I hold your hand in spirit. It is not the same, but it's the best I can offer. Others don't know how to do this. They say, 'You are lucky. Your mom has an open, encompassing heart, one filled with joy for the life you had. One filled with grief, but open for the love.' If people only knew the answers when they were there (on earth) they wouldn't destroy themselves. Your sun is mine, Mom. I'm in a place where all is good, there is no evil. There is sunshine and brightness. Light filled. These things are here because God loves us all. It is all in the plan."

JANICE

Oct. 18, 2010:

"I am winsome, like a feather touching your cheek, like a crisp morning breeze you feel on your face. Like a banded scent of roses, like a journey in your imagination. You have a smile emerge on your face when I'm near. I like that. Create a safe place in your heart for us to exist, where you know I'll always be. Your little slice of Heaven. Lauren with the big brown eyes; they saw beyond your eyes and into your heart. See me, Mom. Feel me, love me. I catch your wishes and turn them into dreams. Spell my name in the air, and I will come, for my significance is amazing. It takes a lot for me to get to you. I'm good at it. I am blessed because of our love. I paddle my way through channels to you."

"I can't imagine it's easy for you to get to me," I said.

"I have ways. I pave roads so I can get to you. Waves of energy flow through me. Sparks of light are all around me. It would be surreal for me to explain to you how it is where I am. Windows to get to you, openings, pure love brings It. "I possess things that are very hard to explain to you. You'll see it disclosed in many ways. In wishes coming true. Others surprising you with their kindness, doors opening, hearts jumping for joy. People getting your message. I will try to carry you forward through your days. I am a believer in God and his wonder. I see the inner workings now. The scale of which all of us can't comprehend. A divinity of clarity beyond measure. A source so bright that you can't even imagine. Perpetual where I am. No beginning, no end. Eternity. Allowing daughters to come to mothers like

I am now. I witness things here like you wouldn't believe. Miracles, gentle kindness, forgiveness, rationality, patience, wonderment, allowing. Graciousness of God in his presence. Me saying, 'Wow, I thought I was happy there, but this is really something.'"

"You're beautiful, Laur."

"I'm more beautiful in light, Mom, because I've ascended, and from that I've learned to share and give back from you and your work, and your spirit, and your giving and caring ways."

"You are my gem, Laurie."

"A diamond, Mom, a diamond that will last forever. I'm going to say goodbye now, but I'm always here. Enjoy life. Baba says so, too. Souls touch."

✦

I have been receiving messages from Lauren for more than four years, but I never really knew if these messages were meant to be shared with others. At the same time, I never wanted to tell anyone because the messages were sacred to me. I didn't want Lauren's messages to become idle gossip, nor did I want our interaction to end. I was concerned that sharing the messages might somehow be exploiting Lauren, which I would never do. If she wanted others to know, I thought, she would certainly tell me.

But I felt as if I was carrying a huge secret that needed to be told. Now, after time has passed, I realized not telling Lauren's friends and family about the messages would be unfair to them. Why should I be the only one to know Lauren's doing fine; that she is happy and whole after the horrific ordeal she experienced? It would be selfish on my part if I never shared Lauren's messages of hope and peace with others who had lost loved ones. It would be selfish to not share with non-believers the beauty and gifts of life after death.

But I couldn't share the messages I received until I directly heard from Lauren that this was the path she wanted me to pursue.

"I have an agenda that I'm asking you to follow. It's about your breadth and scope of it. Expansion of your soul's purpose. To bring a message of hope, and not despair. To create loving words of kindness and compassion. Wisdom to others. Knowledge about what I've gone through. About heartfelt times for you; your ups, your downs, your tears, your joy, your sorrow and your pain. Your enlightenment and awareness. Your journey is far from over. You can't imagine the roads you will encounter. Heights you never thought you'd reach. Sunsets of love. Development of criteria. Betterment of others. Speak words of wisdom. Choreography of a life of love (meaning of her life). *Mom, you're a source for delivering messages to others in a way that only you could tell it because you're brave; gutsy. You can do it. Don't let anyone put you down. You have courage beyond belief. You survived this and you are coming out like a lady.*

Although I understood the importance of what Lauren wanted me to do, I still resisted. Lauren immediately contacted Debbie because she knew what I was feeling in my heart: "I don't want to tell our story I just want my girl back; I want to live a normal life."

*"Mom's had her ups and downs. Wishes she could see me.
I have a job to do. Believe in yourself. Open your eyes
to the possibilities. Build awareness within. Create more
thoughts that are positive, Mom. Send your wishes to the
sky, I will catch them. I will devour your words and help
you write. I will help dissect and plan. It's my process too. I
want others to know how I feel. Open your hearts to a story
of love not defeat. Create more things that are positive.
Give help to those who suffer. There's truth and wisdom in
my knowledge and for others to seek truth in my wisdom.
I am the author. Some pen I have. You have a burning
desire to be free of the pain, but this is your journey, and
you're handling it beautifully. And I am applauding you
for that. You're my star, Mom. One who worries, but
laughs and lets you get away with things. I challenged you
and I still will. I'll give you the little nudge you need to get
you going on things."*

With every message from Lauren, I realized that there was
no turning back.

"Surprise visitors around your book."

When Lauren said that I began thinking to myself, "What
does she mean?" Lauren heard me, of course:

*"Don't try and figure it out, Mom. It is future stuff. Those
who believed in me still do. My friends will know it's me
talking. You will be a source of their growth, their awakening. The reason why I was in their lives will be revealed
to them. Jubilation will be yours. I will be a star. It will be
the revealed purpose of life, of love driving everything. A*

teaching. I was ordinary there, doing good things, but now that I've passed I will be listened to. Now I'll get people's attention. About looking at life in a different way. About opening your heart, being as present as you can. Engaging with people. Listening to their song. Wisdom. Your journey of faith and healing.

"I see the book in a book jacket. It's a triumph for you, Mom. My magic comes through you. I help your fingers slide across the keyboard. I am proud of who you are. I help bring your life to a crescendo. A beautiful opening of your inner spirit. Your love, your laughter, your sadness your grief on pages. A brave courageous journey of sharing beyond belief. A way to let others know there is no end. Treasures can't be buried, they just go on. We sign on for these things when we get to the earth plane. I signed on for this. I did it gracefully and now I have risen.

"I'm whole, Mom, don't worry. I'm still yours, but shared with God. As it should be. I'm from pure love and we shared that. On wings of angels, I am allowed to come back. I am in an existence with nature. In the unfolding of flowers. In the sights and sounds of beautiful places. I am free. I have wings of an angel. They started to grow when I was there."

33

Janice

Infinity is a word Carli introduced to our family vocabulary when she was just a little girl. I was washing dishes and I remember her running into the house. She tugged on my shirt. When I turned around to see what she wanted, I saw her beautiful toothless smile, and she said, "Mommy, I love you "ffffffffinity!" After that, I began signing my cards and letters to the girls, "Infinity, Mom."

I mentioned to Carli that if I were to ever write a book about our experience with Lauren it would be titled *Infinity*. The title was such an appropriate description of what had been happening in my life, and a word that often had been used by me and my girls when they lived at home.

When Lauren announced during a channeling session with Debbie that the title of the book would be *Infinity*, a chill ran through me, from my head to my toe. A ball of heat and energy also engulfed Debbie. The moment was magical, transporting me to a whole different place in my life. Lauren explained:

"You are beginning a journey. One that is filled with chal-

lenges, but you can handle it. Writing a book. Windows of opportunity. My voice will be booming through the book. A way to touch many through my teachings. Carli is not the only teacher. Infinity. Walls of doubt will come down. Skeptics will contemplate the possibility. My friends will know it's me speaking.

"Kernels of wisdom will emerge. Ways to help people to deal with death. Infinity, Mom…Messages will be written by me. Correlations will be made. Silence will emerge into knowing. Create your own way of profiling a tragedy into wisdom. A source of healing for others. (Sacred). It will create a balance in your life. A way of knowing what others don't know about. A correspondence with God. A feeling of life not ending, a transition of joy and beauty. Where wisdom grows and flourishes. Work still being done for souls of others.

"How do you like how smart I sound, Mom? I am a creator of goodwill. I bring people together. I bring smiles and tears. I open their hearts in ways of loving and thinking of their own family and how important they are and to spend more time with them. That is my message. I chose you because I knew you could do it. I knew you had the strength.

On Nov. 20, 2010, Lauren contacted Debbie:

"My pen is from afar. A journey to teach others. A work through the crime to a triumph of love. My job is to let you know you are vessels of love. Triumphant women who are doing a brave job. No housewives of the western suburbs, you two are superstars. I love you both. Mom, kick ass!

⊘∾

One Saturday, Debbie and I were talking on the telephone, sharing our doubts about writing this book because of the skeptics we knew we'd encounter. Still, we wanted to pursue our project. Lauren obviously heard us talking because the very next day, she contacted Debbie. Debbie later told me she knew Lauren had something to say because she strongly sensed her presence. She asked Lauren whether she needed her and Lauren reaffirmed Debbie's intuitive instincts.

Lauren's message was poignant and direct. She reminded us who was in charge of the project and Lauren's orders were quite clear and rather humorous:

> *"Back open a window of faith in yourselves. Hurry to get this done. Hearts to heal. Grief of mothers, but to show them how she (Mom) got through things. How she keeps going. Packages came to her in insight. Like putting your foot on a gas pedal, you (Mom) just keep going. Echoing of her sentiments (Lauren). Bombardment of the truth. A tragedy meaning assisting others in their grief.*

> *"Set your sails high, girls. You're on a ride of a lifetime. Don't hold back, Debbie. I am going to take you girls on a trip. I'm in the driver's seat. A copy of my Mom's heart's wishes. Freedom of the pain; a vacation from the sorrow. We're a team now, like we were. You have no choice now, ladies. You're in this. A pretty strong force, huh guys?*

> *"Bolster my spirit, sometimes I need it. Fade yourself a path of skeptics, don't worry about them. Those who 'get it' will get it, and those who are hindered will be getting*

*a lesson. Deliver this to her (Mom) A map of angels, a cry
in the night to be eased. A daughter to help mothers. To
console, Jan."*

We realized there was no turning back. My daughter had a
plan for us and I hoped to never disappoint her. I had to ensure
that her life was not lived nor taken in vain.

∾⳽⳾∾

I was very excited to contact Lauren and share with her:

"I'm finished with the manuscript for the book," I
told her.

*"Do you believe you did it? With my help. I'm the brains
of the outfit. A little twinkle in your eye that makes your
pen work. Have you told my friends yet?"*

"No, but I will tell them. I will tell Megan and Dory
first because they are coming to visit me."

*"Megan will cry. Dory will be more quiet about it. They'll
believe because they know me. Who's to question? I can still
shock them. Still have an impact. My friends are anxious
to hear about me. Please tell them. They will be honored."*

"I will make sure they know, I promise."

I worked up the nerve to keep my promise to tell Lauren's
friends with whom I had remained in close contact during
the past four years. I studied their faces as I shared some of
Lauren's messages. I couldn't help thinking to myself, "Come

on Laur, help me out because they will think I'm crazy." Lauren heard me and responded immediately. The dining room lights dimmed very low and then shone very brightly. It happened on two different occasions. Lauren's friends all witnessed it, and they were so amazed and enlightened.

During a later channeling session with Debbie, Lauren told me:

"I think it's good that you shared. Not easy, but it's good. Carli thought you should. I'm a champ. My girls, they need to know I'm fine. They need to know my wishes for them to be fine with this whole mess they had to go through. Their memories of me need to be in the glory that I am. I want them to have good memories of me when I was there and good memories of who I am now, not the tragedy. I want them to move on from this."

❧

I still see Lauren's oldest friends – Steph, Meg, Dory, Jill and Julie. Lauren's "partners in crime" recently came to my house for dinner. It was a gloomy day and the sky was very dark as we ate dinner at my dining room table. I handed the girls the latest transcript from Valentine's Day 2011, but as always, they asked me to read it aloud because it made them feel closer to Lauren. As I shared Lauren's message, the sun began to shine brightly through my blinds. The blinds were so illuminated with light that it was as if the sun was attempting to push its way into my house.

Jill jumped up from the table and reached for the blinds' cord. "Can we open the blinds?" she asked excitedly.

The sun shone even brighter. It was so bright we couldn't see for a few seconds. The girls were shouting and commenting on the sun's brightness on such a gloomy day, and it was after 7 p.m.

"Look at the clouds," Steph suddenly yelled. "It's the angel on the water!"

In the sky was the cloud formation that I first witnessed and photographed in North Carolina in 2007 (*see photos*). Almost simultaneously, the girls became excited. A couple of them said: "Oh, my God" and "I have the chills." When we sat at the dining room table again, the sun seemed to shine even more brightly. It was a beautiful moment that Lauren and I got to share with her friends Once again, I stood there looking in amazement, and I thanked my daughter for all she continues to do for me.

The next day, I went to Debbie's for a channeling session and I asked Lauren:

"Did you show the girls the sun last night?"

"A messenger in light. Rays in the shape of me. Sadness in their hearts will lighten. Their lives will go on. Holes in their hearts from Laurie will lessen. They are in awe. Yeah, like the little blonde can do this. I cracked them up."

"The girls and I talked about how we didn't suffer enough," I said.

"No one needed to. It was my journey. Turn it around and send out love to everyone and don't dwell on that. We're all in this together. The girls have their lives to live and should experience joys in their own special way. The funny stories they tell about me, the laughter, the tears."

34

Janice

Lauren continues to remind me of the importance of sharing our story:

> *"It's about tragedy turned into hope and caring. My work, as I see it, needs to be done through you, Mom, with your strength to withstand a life without me. Through you, I have a voice now, my crusader, my loving mother. To show them that Spirit does exist. To cite that love is everlasting for those who want to believe. A speaker of truths, of wisdom gained from where I am at. Paralysis in people's hearts will begin to open. We are co-authors. Silence would have been easier, I know, but how could I have reached you then? I need to feel your touch in words and ways that we share.*

> *"From love, a gift from God. Patience and knowing that we will be together again someday. Not to be feared, but to create a balance in the universe. To create a feeling of purpose, to sail through a cloud of intelligence, to bring pieces from experiences to say we can do this. To willfully*

know that there is more after here to pay back."

I realize now why Lauren was taken so young. She had such a great impact on so many people. It was clear that her legacy needed to continue, and so she made plans for me and Debbie to help bring her story to light. Rather than a story about a murder and a brilliant life that ended too soon, Lauren's message and mission is one of hope. She is showing and sharing that there is life, joy and beauty after death:

June, 9, 2011:

"Tortured souls really need to sort things out and run through everything when they get here. It's a stepped process. The power is ours when we are on earth, but not everyone realizes it, to make the best choices."

To those who have experienced the loss of a child, or anyone they love dearly, Lauren's messages and contact with me demonstrates the infinite power of love that knows no boundaries. I'm living proof of how my daughter's guidance and compassion helped me begin to heal and make sense of a tragedy that could have destroyed my life. But because of Lauren's courage to push beyond the barriers and beliefs of what we've been taught about death, we are all now living proof of Infinity.

JANICE

"I am a whisper of a girl, creating a roar!"
Lauren
Mothers' Day 2011

"Hollar!"

Epilogue:
Lauren, Debbie and Janice

From Lauren's "Vision Essay," June 2005 (written prior to her passing):

"As I look at my life, I realize that I have been through many obstacles. Some were hard times, and others were the best times of my life. I also know that I have shared these moments with the people I am closest to. My family, friends, and God have supported me. As I grow older, my life is coming together and through my experiences, my loved ones have not only taught me things, but I have learned a great deal from them as well as many lessons on my own. The song, 'I Hope You Dance,' is a song that is very important to me. Whenever I have been upset or happy, this song always seems to come on at the right time. It gives me hope and I can relate it to my life."

From Lauren, channeled in 2010:

"Resting in a place of glory, in peace and tranquility. It almost feels how it did when I was in a fetal position inside you. It's that peaceful, Mom. The peace is unimaginable. I get to do, be, feel and say whatever I want. I am a teacher. My priority is you, and I know the book will help heal you. It is a conscious triumph of our everlasting love over an inconceivable act. We weave words together to help others. Special stories of our love conveyed to all. In humor and in sadness. To instill in others to have hope. To say not everyone's journey lasts a lifetime. I speak in honor of my family. Aware of the pride and joy of who I am...the love that shaped me."

From Lauren, channeled in 2011:

"It's so different where I am, no social. No way to explain it. In a world where everything is beautiful. Everything is heightened. Worries gone, no judgment, no lies, no horror, no persecution, no prejudice, no spite, no cruelty, no weather. Solitude in the most incredible way. Peace beyond belief. Reality unlike there. Waves of consciousness. Stepping between worlds.

"I crawled through tunnels to come back to share this knowledge, to share this peace. In incomprehensible ways, I'm touching, evolving, moving, sharing, creating...culminating peace. Changing people's lives, opening hearts, letting others see into the light of my life. How impactful one person can be to see the potential in all. To never under estimate yourself. My lessons will be felt by many. I share information, love, goodwill, joy. I see through peo-

ple's sorrow to bring them joy. To offer them an alternative to crying. To smile when they think about their loved ones who have passed. To know they are in a place of peace, comfort, joy…surrounded…wholesome."

From Debbie:

I still shake my head in disbelief when I think about the incredible events surrounding the extraordinary and eternal life of Lauren Kiefer. If I hadn't been personally involved and engaged in the journey, I wouldn't have believed everything that has happened these past four years. I feel blessed that Lauren and the Universe, in its infinite wisdom, chose me to be the channel for this tragic, yet heroic and profound journey. Looking back, I can only feel joy for having been a witness to this almost incomprehensible story of unconditional and eternal love.

I never "knew" Lauren on this side of Earth's plane. From photos, I could see that she was physically beautiful. But I had the humbling experience of getting to know the beauty of her spirit – the spirit that persevered to reach her grieving mother, Janice, and provide help and guidance from the other side.

The power and vitality of Lauren's essence shone through from the first moment we made contact. I found it amazing that after the brutality she experienced on that Christmas Evening 2006, Lauren's main concern was for her mother's well-being. She was grateful her mother had not experienced what she had endured that night. Because of Lauren's unconditional love for Janice and compassionate heart towards her mother's suffering, Lauren has given us all a glimpse of her life on the other side, and insight into how we all will ascend into the Light.

The thread that weaves throughout Lauren's life is the triumph of her spirit. While another person's sadness and self-loathing took her physical body away, he could not destroy the truth of Lauren's life. Her light could not be dimmed by an act of violence. The energy of spirit never dies. The energy of love cannot be destroyed.

As I reflect on Lauren's life, I can't help but see her as an enlightened messenger whose spirit – while she was here, as well as where she is now – is one of pure love. Her indomitable spirit and contagious joy could never be curtailed by a tragic event, and Lauren has navigated a path unimaginable to most of us in order to share her messages of infinite love and hope for all of us to cherish and celebrate.

I thank Lauren for opening the gate and leading me on a compelling and life-changing passage to the truth of life's eternity. I'm so grateful for the beautiful lessons I have learned. I'm also grateful to you, the reader, for sharing this journey with us. Your support helps reaffirm the powerful and everlasting connection that links all of us to each other, and heralds the pure, loving bond between a mother and daughter that transforms any and everyone who reads this book.

Lauren, thank you for not "sitting it out," and for sharing with us the beautiful dance of your eternal soul.

From Janice:

As I reflect on the tragedy that has defined the last four years of my life, I still can't believe that my daughter's life was taken at such a young age during a senseless crime. Yet, some part of me believes Lauren's passing was all in the "plan" that was decided a long time ago. As she once told me during a channeling session:

*"A moment, Mom, we had a moment, and now we have
eternity."*

I can't begin to express enough gratitude to Debbie and
Lauren for seeing me through to the place where I am today.
Without Lauren's love and determination, and Debbie's self-
lessness, I would have never made it through this horrific time.
I feel so blessed to still have Lauren in my life, and to have been
chosen to receive this wondrous gift.

My Dearest Lauren:

*I love and miss you more than words can say. Thank you
for guiding me with your beautiful light. I couldn't do it
without you…you know. You've brought me to a place I've
never dreamt possible. You've made me a believer, and I
live by your words because my once little scatterbrained
daughter is wise way beyond her years.*

*Since you've been gone, you have taught me more than I
could ever learn in an entire lifetime. You are not only my
daughter and friend, but you are my soulmate, teacher,
keeper, mentor, my strength. You are my hero! I feel closer
to you now than I ever have. We're a team. Two peas in a
pod. You have brought me from the deepest darkness into
the brightest light. You have taught me the true meaning
of "Infinity" and that pure love never dies; it only becomes
stronger, even in death, if you allow it to. You've taught me
to see the "bigger picture" and to not sweat the small stuff because we are only passing through. You've taught me to know
that life is a gift, and to make the most of it while I'm here.
You've taught me to be kind to others that are less fortunate,*

and to know that we will be together again someday.

Here is your book sweetheart, filled with your amazing wisdom. You were my challenge on earth, and you are still challenging me from where you are. I hope I have fulfilled your wishes in bringing your message of hope to others. I'm just wondering, as always, where are you taking me now??

Until we meet again…

I love you INFINITY,
Your Mom
xoxoxoxoxo

Acknowledgements

From Jan:

Precious Lauren, thank you for showing me your caring, infinite love, wisdom, and light from another place. You are truly a miracle and a wonderful daughter that I will treasure always.

Dearest Carli, thank you for staying strong; keeping me grounded, and bringing me back to life in spite of your own grief and the loss of your precious sister and friend.

Thank you, to my wonderful family and friends, who have seen me through this most difficult time.

Thank you, Tiffany, for going above and beyond the call of duty to help me.

Special thanks to Steve and Sara for your support in the production of this book.

To Susan and Mary Jo, thank you for your generosity.

And to Debbie, there are no words…

From Debbie:

Fantastic journeys are born of and evolve from innumerable sources. My journey was the gift from a soul I never met on this side, but whom I now feel has become the gift of another daughter. Thank you, Lauren.

Thank you, Jan, for sharing your friendship and love. You can move mountains when you set your mind to it! You are amazing.

My daughters – my teachers, my guides. I wish to thank my first-born, Erica, for sharing with me your short physical life in order to guide me to the eternal light in which you reside. You led me to awaken to a higher plane of intuitive knowing of pure love and provided me with an unexpected vision of my life's purpose. You taught me that disguised in the depths of tragedy is hope and rebirth.

To my dearest daughter Erin, who also decided to arrive prematurely, I extend my deepest gratitude. You are wise beyond measure. I'm so grateful that you chose me as your mother. You have shone the way for me and countless others through your compassionate and conscious living. I love you so!

Loving thanks to my parents, Guido and Doris Smania, who provided the loving environment from which I grew, making it possible to ask questions and spread my wings.

I thank my beloved dog Sadie, whose own gentle spirit has served as a guidepost for my soul.

For all of my family, friends and guides in the physical and non-physical world who continue to support me with love and understanding, I thank you.

Thanks to Jeff Sahagian, whose persistence led to the unfolding of this amazing phenomenon – my contact with Lauren. You pushed me out of my comfort zone and touched many lives through your efforts.

Thanks to Detective Tiffany Wayda and the DuPage County Sheriff's Department whose compassion, tenacity and dedication helped to bring a sense of peace to a grieving mother.

Warm thanks to Jeri Love, whose patience is beyond measure. You adeptly organized the voice of three souls who came to you with their unusual tale of love. You helped us bring Lauren's voice to many. You truly live up to your surname.

And to all who will read this book, thank you. It's our hope that you will take away from it exactly what you need to heal, open your mind, and experience the awe and wonder of life's eternal and infinite majesty, mystery and magic.

Resources You May Also Find Helpful

http://www.infinitylauren.com
Infinity Web Site

http://www.remberlaur.com
Lauren Kiefer Memorial Foundation

http://www.intuitivereikienergy.com

http://www.thecompassionatefriendsfw.com
Compassionate Friends

http://www.pomac.com
Parents of Murdered Children

On Grief and Grieving by David Kessler and Elisabeth
  Kubler-Ross

Hello From Heaven by Bill and Judy Guggenheim

CPSIA information can be obtained at www.ICGtesting.com
Printed in the USA
LVOW060751240112

265249LV00002B/3/P